MODEL POLICIES FOR SMALL AND MEDIUM PUBLIC LIBRARIES

JEANETTE LARSON AND HERMAN L. TOTTEN

NEAL-SCHUMAN PUBLISHERS, INC.

NEW YORK

Published by Neal-Schuman Publishers
100 Varick Street
New York, NY 10013

Printed in the United States of America.

Library of Congress Cataloging-in-Publication Data

Larson, Jeanette.
   Model policies for small and medium public libraries / by Jeanette Larson and Herman L. Totten.
       p.   cm.
   Includes bibliographical references and index.
   ISBN 1-55570-343-7
   1. Public libraries—United States—Administration. 2. Small libraries—United States—Administration. I. Totten, Herman L. II. Title.
   Z678.L28 1998
   025.174—dc21   98-7917
                                                      CIP

Contents

Master List of Model Policies   vii
Acknowledgments   ix
Preface   xi

Chapter 1: Policies and Their Importance   **1**

What Are Policies?   1
Why Are Policies and Policy Manuals Important?   2
Where and How Do Policies Originate?   4
What Are the Legalities of Policies?   5

Chapter 2: How to Develop Policies   **9**

Determining When to Develop Policies   9
Developing Effective Policies   10
Steps in Policy Development   11
Policy Manuals and Distribution   14
How to Use Model Policies   15

Chapter 3: Personnel and Employment Practices   **17**

Recruitment of Candidates for Positions   18
Nepotism   20
Staff Development   22
Performance Evaluation and Salary Increases   24
Employee Benefits   27
Use of Volunteers   30
Termination of Employment   32

Chapter 4: Staff Conduct — 35

Code of Ethics — 35
Dress Code — 38
Staff Use of Library Materials and Equipment — 40
Selling and Soliciting in the Library — 42
Political Activities by Employees — 43
Discounts on Staff Book Purchases — 44
Staff Relations and Celebrations — 45

Chapter 5: Access to Library Services — 49

Americans with Disabilities Act — 49
Public Participation in Library Decision Making — 51
Hours of Operation — 53
Public Use of Microcomputers — 55
Internet Access — 57
Library Programs — 61

Chapter 6: Use of Materials — 65

Registration of Patrons — 65
Confidentiality of Library Patron Records — 67
Fees for Services — 72
Fines and Recovery of Overdue Materials — 73
Reciprocal Borrowing Privileges — 76
Interlibrary Loan — 77
Protection of Copyright — 81

Chapter 7: Collection Development — 85

Selection of Materials — 85
Gifts — 88
Materials in Languages Other than English — 93
Request for Reconsideration of Materials — 95
Deselection of Materials — 99

Chapter 8: Reference and Information Services — 103

Reference and Information Services — 103
Homework Assistance — 108
Faxing — 109

Photocopying   111
Database Searching   112
Internet Use Policy   115

Chapter 9: Access and Use of Facilities   125

Use of Meeting Rooms   125
Exhibits and Display Cases   129
Distribution of Free Materials   132
Religious Programming and Decorations   133

Chapter 10: Patron Conduct   137

Library Behavior   137
Unattended Children   139
Harassment and Lewd Behavior   143
Patron Use of Library Supplies   144
Theft of Materials   146

Appendix A: Codes of Ethics   149

American Library Association Code of Ethics   149
Ethics Statement for Public Library Trustees   151

Appendix B: Guidelines for the Development
and Implementation of Policies, Regulations, and
Procedures Affecting Access to Library Materials,
Services, and Facilities   153

Introduction   153
Guidelines   154

Appendix C: *Library Bill of Rights* and Interpretations
of the *Library Bill of Rights*   157

The Library Bill of Rights   157
Statement on Labeling   159
Challenged Materials   161
Free Accesss to Libraries for Minors   162
Library Initiated Programs as a Resource   164
Diversity in Collection Development   166
Access for Children and Young People to
    Videotapes and Other Non-Print Formats   168

Meeting Rooms   170
Exhibit Spaces and Bulletin Boards   172
Economic Barriers to Information Access   174
Evaluating Library Collections   177
Access to Electronic Information, Services, and Networks   178
Resolution on the Use of Filtering Software in Libraries   182

Appendix D: Guidelines for the Development of
Policies and Procedures Regarding User Behavior and
Library Usage   183

Introduction   183
Guidelines   184

Appendix E: Policies on Confidentiality   187

Policy on Confidentiality of Library Records   187
Suggested Procedures for Implementing Policy
    on Confidentiality of Library Records   189
Policy Concerning Confidentiality of Personally
    Identifiable Information about Library Users   190

Appendix F: The Freedom to Read   193

Appendix G: Freedom to View   199

Appendix H: Roles for Public Libraries   201

Bibliography   205

Index   209

About the Authors   213

Master List of Model Policies

Chapter 3: Personnel and Employment Practices

Personnel and Employment Practices   18
Recruitment of Candidates for Positions   20
Nepotism   22
Staff Development   25
Performance Evaluations and Salary Increases   28
Employee Benefits   29
Use of Volunteers   31
Termination of Employment   33

Chapter 4: Staff Conduct

Code of Ethics   37
Dress Code   40
Staff Use of Library Materials and Equipment   41
Selling and Soliciting in the Library   43
Political Activities by Employees   44
Discounts on Staff Book Purchases   45
Staff Relations and Celebrations   46

Chapter 5: Access to Library Services

Americans with Disabilities Act   52
Public Participation in Library Decision Making   54
Hours of Operation   55
Public Use of Microcomputers   58
Internet Access   60
Library Programs   63

Chapter 6: Use of Materials

Registration of Patrons   68
Confidentiality of Library Patron Records   71
Fees for Service, 1   74
Fees for Service, 2   74
Fines and Recovery of Overdue Materials   76
Reciprocal Borrowing Privileges   78
Interlibrary Loan   80
Protection of Copyright   82

Chapter 7: Collection Development

Selection of Materials   89
Gifts   94
Materials in Languages Other than English   96
Request for Reconsideration of Materials   98
Deselection of Materials   100

Chapter 8: Reference and Information Services

Reference and Information Services   106
Homework Assistance   109
Faxing   111
Photocopying   113
Database Searching   115
Internet Use   122

Chapter 9: Access and Use of Facilities

Use of Meeting Rooms, 1   128
Use of Meeting Rooms, 2   129
Exhibits and Display Cases, 1   131
Exhibits and Display Cases, 2   132
Distribution of Free Materials   134
Religious Programming and Decorations   135

Chapter 10: Patron Conduct

Library Behavior   140
Unattended Children   142
Harassment and Lewd Behavior   144
Patron Use of Library Supplies   145
Theft of Materials   147

Acknowledgments

This book is the result of requests from many colleagues and clients who wanted to see samples of policies prepared by other libraries. Many people helped with suggestions, questions, and comments but special thanks must go to Julie Todaro for reading early versions of each policy and making helpful and insightful suggestions. It would also have been impossible to finish the manual without the help of Anne Ramos, Library Science Librarian at the Texas State Library. Her diligent searches for sample policies, documents, and background information prevented numerous errors or omissions. Other colleagues and staff members, aware of this project, read specific policies, provided copies of interesting articles or sample policies, and supported our efforts. John Corbin read several chapters making valuable suggestions for refining their content and Barbara Stein was always patient, but persistent, in her support for the book.

In order to provide model policies, rather than simply reprint samples from a variety of libraries, we looked at many documents to find common threads, trends in language, and consensus in issues. Libraries and staff that sent policy manuals, sample policies, or responded to requests for other information or comments must be acknowledged for sharing their experience. In some cases we are not sure who on the library's staff sent information but we are grateful that they did. These people and libraries include:

Christopher Bowen, Downers Grove (IL) Public Library
Brenda Branch, Austin (TX) Public Library
Peg Bredeson, Beloit (WI) Public Library

James Cook, Dayton & Montgomery County Public Library, Dayton, OH

Helen Dunbar, Alameda (CA) County Library

Elsie Dunlap, Bettendorf (IA) Public Library

Charlene Edmundson, Northeast Texas Library System, Garland, TX

Beth Fox, Westbank Community Library, Austin, TX

Ann Gault, Val Verde County Library, Del Rio, TX

Rose Aleta Laurell, Dr. Eugene Clark Library, Lockhart, TX

Oakland (CA) Public Library

Onondaga County Public Library, Syracuse, NY

Connie Pottle, Memphis Shelby County Public Library, Memphis, TN

Mary Lee Smith, Lovington (NM) Public Library

Nancy Smith, King County Public Library, Seattle, WA

Lamar Veatch, Irving (TX) Public Library

Yvonne Chandler kept Herman's computer running and made sure that different software packages were compatible. Finally, I must thank my husband, James W. Larson, for his constant help with my computer problems, his gentle reminders that I get back to work on this book, and his overall support for my work.

Preface

Model Policies for Small and Medium Public Libraries was specifically designed for the directors and staff of small- and medium-sized public libraries who know that they need policies but are uncertain which policies will best serve their library. It will also be especially useful for the one-person library where there is no staff with whom to discuss issues. While the terms "small" and "medium" have a variety of interpretations, we wrote this book with libraries serving populations of under 100,000 people in mind.

Most of us acknowledge the need for current, relevant, useful policies, yet many librarians put off developing new policies or revising old ones because it can be a time-consuming, and sometimes controversial, process. This book provides a systematic way to explore the policies already in place in your library, revise those that need to be updated, and develop policies that may be needed, but are missing in your organization. Having an outline to follow may move the process forward. Because policy development and revision is most frequently initiated and carried forward by the library director, we frequently refer to "you" when discussing issues to be considered. Although the realities of the workplace may result in a lot of the work being performed by one or two people, it is wise to involve staff members, volunteers, board members, and others in the process. These are the policies of the library and they "articulate the library's position on matters of philosophy and operations."[1] As such, they should be the result of input and review by others who are affected by the policies or who must carry them out or support them.

There is also the commonly held viewpoint that policies become outdated as soon as they are set on paper. While this often may be true, it is unwise to put off developing policies just because they may have to be changed in a year. In fact, as you will see in Chapter 2, policies should be reviewed and revised on a regular schedule. Knowing what issues need to be explored will help you develop policies that do not become quickly outdated and will facilitate updating policies when necessary. Word processors and computers make it so much easier to revise a few policies and reprint them every year or so, avoiding the onerous situation of having to revise every policy at the same time.

The model policies provided can serve as patterns or examples for you to use in developing your own policies. Many library directors are concerned that they cannot develop policies from scratch. Others feel more comfortable with a model policy from which to build their local policy. The primary way in which many librarians develop policy is by collecting samples from other libraries and copying the parts that seem to best match the needs of their library. While it is certainly useful to examine what other libraries are doing, that is not the end of your research! This book explores the issues and raises questions that must be resolved locally if the policies developed are to be useful and supportable. Avoid the "cut-and-paste" method and the result will be policies that best suit the needs of your community and the roles and abilities of your library. Librarians who do not have immediate access to legal counsel will also find this handbook to be a useful resource for developing ideas before seeking counsel.

WHAT POLICIES ARE INCLUDED?

We have attempted to include most of the policies that would be useful for small- and medium-sized libraries. These include policies for personnel and employment practices, library services, collection development, copyright, Internet access, intellectual freedom, and library programs. We have also included policies for staff and patron conduct, special collections, reference services, and use of resources.

Not every library needs or wants every one of the policies we have included. While there are general policies that every library may want to have immediately, such as a collection development policy, other policies will not be immediately required. For example, why have a policy on staff use of library vehicles if you do not have a library vehicle or if the staff is so small that use or potential misuse has not created any problems? Furthermore, some libraries may find the need for additional policies not included in this book. The bibliography at the end of this book offers titles that will provide guidance in developing those policies.

Policies covering some specific areas are essential. If no policies currently exist in written form, the first priority should be to develop one to comply with the Americans with Disabilities Act, a policy on copyright, a policy on reconsideration of materials, and one on patron behavior. It is also recommended that an Internet policy be in place before you initiate public access. These policies can be revised and refined as you become more familiar with your library and community or as problems and situations develop. They are, however, the policies that will provide some protection to you and the library from possible legal action and from situations that may result in poor public relations.

WHAT IS NOT INCLUDED?

While we have attempted to include models of most policies that a small- or medium-sized library might need, we have specifically not included a policy on sexual harassment. This area has become well defined by case and legal precedents. Therefore, most parent institutions have well-articulated sexual harassment policies in place for every entity within their political jurisdiction. If the legal structure of your library is such that you are not a part of a larger political entity, then you will want to refer to *The Librarian's Legal Companion*[2] and develop a harassment or sexual harassment policy for your library. You might also refer to the Spring 1997 issue of *Illinois Libraries* for a ten-step program to minimize the likelihood of sexual harassment and reduce the likelihood of lawsuits.[3]

WHAT INFORMATION IS PROVIDED?

When it comes to library policies, one size will never fit all! While it might be tempting to exactly copy policies from other libraries, that is not a good course of action. Your library is not exactly the same as another and your patrons' needs may be very different from those of another library. It is also best to avoid the inclination to cut-and-paste, using policies from several libraries to try to develop a policy that suits your needs. Obviously, we are also not advocating that anyone circumvent the process of deliberation and decision making outlined in this book and simply copy the model policies we have provided. Chapter 1 discusses the importance of policies and describes how they originate. Part of the origination process includes developing buy-in from staff (including, if relevant, volunteer staff in the one-person or very small library) and from the library's governing authority. For policies to be legal and to withstand local scrutiny if challenged, they must have been carefully thought out. All of the issues should have been thoroughly discussed and understood by the people (staff and governing authority) who must implement and support the policies.

Background

We have provided background information for each model policy. This information defines the problem or addresses the situation for which your library may decide a policy is needed. We have explored areas of concern and have indicated the rationale for developing a policy on the topic. Background information should also help the library's governing authority and any advisory boards or support groups understand why a specific policy may be needed.

In most cases, the background information is succinct, offering a basis upon which you can begin discussion of the issues. The exception to this is in the policy on Internet use in Chapter 8. Because the Internet is still relatively new in libraries, and is an issue that can create a great deal of controversy, the background information is rather lengthy and detailed.

Issues

A number of issues that must be addressed by the library and its staff, board, and governing body as part of developing a policy have been enumerated for consideration. We have tried to be exhaustive in listing and discussing the issues, although we do not claim to have included every possible topic or subtopic that might be included in your discussions. We have examined policies from a variety of different libraries, small and large, to see what issues were included in their policies. We also reviewed books, journal articles, and Internet Web sites to obtain various viewpoints and background on the issues. Publications and Internet sites that were useful or that might provide further background for you are included in the bibliography.

We have pointed out areas where local, state, or federal laws may play a role in the development of your policies. For example, the use of volunteers in the library may be partially governed by union rules and child labor laws. We have indicated areas where you may need to do further research, either in library literature or within your community. For example, it is difficult to set policies on library hours without knowing the community's wishes; therefore, local research is essential. Similarly, it is difficult to establish a policy on unattended children in the library without knowing local and state laws or ordinances dealing with the age at which children can be left unsupervised.

We have also indicated issues that may be influenced by the American Library Association (ALA) and its policies, guidelines, or the ALA Code of Ethics. While the policies or dictates of the American Library Association do not bind local public libraries, that body represents more than 50,000 librarians; in many ways, its policies and guidelines act as the mores for our entire profession. As such, while a local library may choose not to endorse a specific ALA policy or parts of an ALA policy, that decision should be made with full knowledge of how local issues are affected by these national values. When specific concerns of a segment of the local community are at odds with national guidelines or policies, ALA's position on topics of professional concern may strengthen support for policies that further the library's mission and goals. Ultimately, the development of local policies rests with the local governing authority, and not with the American Library Association, state library agencies, or state associations. However, it is useful to know and understand the foundations and philosophies upon which many library services and principles are based. Local decisions can then be made from a position of knowledge and understanding after careful thought and consideration of the issues and their effect on local services.

Local Decisions

Because you will be making local decisions about the policies of your library, be sure to write in this book! Recording decisions made during the deliberation process that precedes proper policy articulation will serve as a record of your decisions. This will assist you and your successors as policies are updated and revised. Library board meetings or meetings of other library governing bodies will, of course, have written minutes to record the final decisions made about policies. Nevertheless, much of the thought process that precedes the presentation of a policy for approval will take place in policy committee meetings, staff meetings, or in solitary contemplation. It is easier to recall why decisions were made if notes have been kept, so keep them in this book.

Model Policies

As a convenience and to provide a starting point for writing, we have provided model policies. Although we examined policies from dozens of libraries and looked at numerous books on the topics for which policies are provided, we did not base the model on any individual policy. In some instances, there was a great deal of similarity in the policies of different libraries, while in other cases the policies we examined varied widely.

While a specific model policy may appear to be a close fit to the needs of your library, the models were not written with any specific representative library in mind. The models are included to offer a representation of how the issues might be decided and to indicate our opinion as to the relative length of the particular policy. Even a brief policy on selection of materials will be much longer than a policy on making photocopies.

We also felt that having a model to serve as a reference point or guide would make the task of developing policies and updating or revising them seem less onerous. We have tried to make your job more achievable. In three instances, two model policies have been provided because resolution of the issues could lead to two totally different policies. For example, some libraries will want a policy that details how fees will be assessed for services that are offered on a cost-recovery basis. Other libraries will establish a brief policy that stipulates that no service will be offered that cannot be paid for through the budget of the library.

Approvals and Signature

Every public library has some governing authority that controls the purse strings and authorizes the existence of the library. It may be a board of trustees, a city council or county commission, or a library board. The members of the governing authority are also the people who will hear the complaints and concerns from angry, upset, or concerned citizens. While some libraries have advisory boards and Friends of the Library groups that may assist them in setting policy, ultimately the authority to implement and enforce a policy rests with the governing authority.

It is important to have advisory and support groups involved in the process of developing policy. However, there is no policy without the approval and attestation of the governing authority. For that reason we have included a statement at the end of each model policy to remind you that the library's governing body *must sign and date the policy*. Without the signatures indicating support, the library staff may find itself without support when a policy is challenged. If the policy for selection of materials indicates that the library will purchase materials that may be in conflict with the views of some segments of the community, gain support for that policy when it is being developed, not in the middle of a censorship battle!

APPENDICES

The appendices include important documents from the American Library Association and its divisions that relate to or support library policies. Because these documents are important in the development of policies for your library, we wanted to present them together. Even if your policy varies from the recommendations indicated in the ALA policy statements, you will want to consider them as you make local decisions.

When your library endorses a specific document or incorporates it into a local policy, it should be referred to in the policy. So that staff and the public have easy access to any ALA documents or policy statements that are accepted by your library, they should be appended to the policy and included in your policy manual.

Because most policies will be established based on the roles selected for your public library, either formally through a planning process or informally through practice, we have also included a summary of the Public Library Association's (PLA) "Roles for Public Libraries." Because it will be referred to frequently and should be used as part of the library's ongoing planning process, we recommend that you purchase the book *Planning & Role Setting for Public Libraries: A Manual of Options and Procedures*.[4] PLA's update and revision of the roles for public libraries was released in April 1998 as *Planning for Results: A Library Transformation Process*. While the emphasis of this new process is on service responses, rather than roles, the concept remains valid: policies are based on the fundamental mission and functions of the library.

NOTES

1. Weingand, Darlene E. *Administration of the Small Public Library*. Chicago: American Library Association, 1992, p. 60.
2. Tryon, Jonathan S. *The Librarian's Legal Companion*. New York: G.K. Hall, 1994.
3. Uhler, Scott F. and Rinda Y. Allison. "A 10-Step Program: Reducing the Likelihood of Sexual Harassment and the Possibility of Successful Sexual Harassment Lawsuits." *Illinois Libraries* 79, no. 2 (Spring 1997): 64-65.
4. McClure, Charles R., et al. *Planning & Role Setting for Public Libraries*. Chicago: American Library Association, 1987.

Chapter 1

Policies and Their Importance

WHAT ARE POLICIES

A policy is a set of guidelines for managerial actions and decisions. While policies may be implied or oral, in recent years increased emphasis has been placed on writing policies that ensure the effective and efficient running of libraries. Policies guide the thinking behind the actions necessary for libraries to achieve their goals and objectives.

Policies can be broad, addressing basic principles that guide the library, or specific, addressing targeted activities. An example of a broad policy would be the materials selection policy that affects materials purchased, received as gifts, or otherwise acquired by the library. "Recruitment of Candidates for Positions" with the library is an example of a specific policy. This policy addresses only the recruitment process but provides very specific guidance for that activity. Policies can also be institution-wide, applicable to all segments of the organization, or department-wide, applicable to a small segment of the organization.

Policies cover a wide range of topics, which can be divided into two groups:

- Managerial policies deal with functions of planning, organizing, staffing, directing, and controlling. For example, a staff development policy might state that all new staff will be rotated through all work areas during their first year.

- Operational policies deal with functions that support the library's service objectives, such as selection and development of resources, finance, and personnel and public relations. For example, an acquisitions policy might state that whenever possible, library materials should be purchased to present various sides of controversial issues.

Procedures, rules, and regulations differ from and are subordinate to policies. Procedures are guides to action: they standardize the methods by which repetitive tasks are performed, usually by listing steps in the order of performance. Rules and regulations provide for uniformity of action in specific situations. They can outline staff and patron behavior through positive (should) and negative (should not) limits, and can provide value (good or bad) constraints. For example, if a library's policy states that non-profit organizations may reserve the meeting room up to ninety days in advance, a subordinate procedure might outline how staff will schedule meeting room use, and a subordinate rule might state how the library will respond to groups that do not cancel their reservations. Procedures and rules must comply with policies and policies should support the implementation and enforcement of the rules and procedures.

WHY ARE POLICIES AND POLICY MANUALS IMPORTANT?

By providing guidelines for decision making, policies ensure some degree of consistency and continuity in the overall administration and day-to-day operation of the library. By reducing uninformed decision making and promoting clarity, policies serve to:

- support the mission, service roles, goals, and objectives of the library;
- clarify relationships and responsibilities within the organization;
- delegate authority by transferring decision making to lower levels of the organization;

- guide acquisitions of library materials; and,
- protect the rights of individuals inside and outside the organization.

All libraries have policies, whether they are written or unwritten, sound or unsound, followed or not followed, understood or not understood, complete or incomplete. It is important to remember that policies can provide freedom as well as restrict it. There are as many cases of frustration within organizations about the lack of policies, procedures, rules, and regulations as there are about arbitrarily established ones. In the absence of policies, each problem must be resolved on its own merit, which leads to decisions—often crisis responses—that can be uninformed, inconsistent, and conflicting. Policies prevent rethinking the same situation, save staff time and energy, and help avoid confusion.

Written policy manuals provide the means for communicating policies to all who are affected by them. Policy manuals are important because they are:

- an invaluable managerial tool for clarifying thinking and guiding decisions by the library board, director, and staff;
- a tangible means of supporting and clarifying the library's objectives and intentions in legal cases;
- a consistent form of internal and external communication, providing direction for day-to-day library operations and service to the community;
- a convenient indoctrination and training tool for new staff members; and
- a public relations tool, demonstrating the library's basic honesty and integrity, protecting rights and ensuring equal treatment of individuals, and generally inspiring confidence in the library's management.

Without a written policy manual, problems and misunderstandings cannot be resolved by reference to a particular set of words or specific language; legal cases may suffer from lack of a critical source of support; and new employees may be confused by misinformation circulating in the organization.

WHERE AND HOW DO POLICIES ORIGINATE?

In many discourses, policy making and decision making are synonymous. Policy making, however, is actually part of decision making: policies emerge from ad hoc decisions and become general statements or understandings that guide thinking in future decision making. The policy-making process involves all levels of the organization, from staff to library board. Governing boards are legally responsible for the operation of the library and usually have their duties spelled out in the library's Articles of Incorporation. Advisory boards are appointed by the political entity of which the library is a department to advise the library director and the local government on various matters. While both types of boards play a direct role in policy development and adoption, as well as providing a means for citizen participation in policy development, the governing board also has responsibility for enforcing library policies. An advisory board may recommend that the city council or county commission approve the policy, and should support library policies, but the governing authority is ultimately responsible for approval and enforcement.

Policies can be categorized four ways, depending on their source:

- *Originated policy* includes policies that flow mainly from library objectives and are formally written and reviewed. Although the policies can originate at any organizational level, actual policy statements are usually drafted by staff and receive final approval from the library's governing authority. Originated policy is the main source of policy making, intended to guide the general operations of the library. An example of this type of policy might be that reference books are for use in the library only.
- *Appealed policy* covers common law, based on decisions made in specific situations, and reinforced over time. Because appealed policies are often made through snap decisions and are rarely given thorough consideration, they can cause tension and confusion. For example, the library director may decide that only certain staff members will receive financial support to attend conferences and workshops, although all staff members need continuing education.

- *Implied policy* develops from actions that employees see repeated and thus assume to be policy. For example, it may appear that children's services staff is not permitted to take vacation time during the summer because of increased workload while students are out of school. It may even be common practice that staff who work with children avoid taking time off when students are out of school. Common practice is not policy; to avoid misunderstandings, staff should be properly briefed on what is and what is not policy.
- *Externally imposed policy* comes from sources outside the organization, such as federal, state, and local laws. Library personnel may have no control over implementing external policies, but must be aware of and incorporate them in the internal policies of the library. For example, the Americans with Disabilities Act is a federal law requiring that libraries make reasonable accommodation to provide services to persons with disabilities.

WHAT ARE THE LEGALITIES OF POLICIES?

Policies provide legal protection and guidance for both staff and users. Library policies must be written in such a way as to withstand judicial procedures and review. Each policy should be discussed with the library's governing authority, which may be a governing board, a city council, or commissioner's court and, if necessary, with the library's legal counsel. Advisory boards and Friends of the Library groups may also be consulted in the development of the policy and will be advocates for the library's policies but have no authority to approve or enforce policies.

The governing authority should approve each policy by signing and dating it. The policy is generally considered operational and legal from the day it is signed until it is revised or deleted. In rare cases, a policy may be approved and distributed to begin as of a certain date. For example, revised policy may limit non-library related use of the meeting room but not be put into effect until after a reasonable amount of time has passed in order to allow groups to make alternative arrangements.

By having each policy attested to separately, the library has better support for the policy and protection if the policy is challenged.

It is easier to get political bodies to endorse policy before there is a problem; it is more difficult to obtain support when tempers and emotions are high. Policies must be consistently re-evaluated to determine whether they should be revised or retained. New laws or legislation, changes in patron needs, new services, etc., may require adjustments to policies or the development of new policies. Additionally, it is a monumental task to try to originate or revise all of the needed policies at once. Having policies updated and developed on an ongoing basis with each policy approved and signed individually breaks the task into manageable segments. This method also allows the governing body to consider fully what they are approving. In case of a complaint about library policy, it is usually better to have the full and informed support of the governing authority. A regularly scheduled plan for reviewing policies also may help you avoid pressure to revise a policy immediately after a conflict or problem has occurred.

Externally imposed policies dictate an action and enforce compliance. For example, state government may require that public libraries retain interlibrary loan records for a period of two years. All publicly supported institutions must abide by the Constitution of the United States and the Amendments to the Constitution, and the laws of their state and local jurisdictions. It is important for library policy makers to stay within the purview of externally imposed laws and policies when developing policies that apply to their personnel and patrons. For example, a decision to close a branch library in order to expand service elsewhere could be challenged on the basis that the closing would jeopardize local citizens' rights to access information.

Generally, library policies should also comply with those of the American Library Association (ALA) and other relevant professional associations or organizations. Policy makers should examine statements such as the ALA's *Library Bill of Rights* to determine whether local policies tend to comply with national policies. When your policies vary from ALA's recommendations, it is important for you and others involved in the process to understand how and why they do not agree. The ALA also provides guidelines for policy makers, such as *Guidelines for the Development of Policies and Procedures Regarding User Behavior and Library Usage* and *Suggested Procedures for Implementing Policy on Confidentiality of Library Records*. These documents, and others you may need for developing policy, are included in the Appendix.

Library policies must be valid and legally enforceable. The State Library of Michigan recommends four validity tests[1] :

1. Legality: Does the policy comply with current laws and statutes of the jurisdiction? All policies should be reviewed to determine their legality.
2. Reasonableness: Is the policy reasonable and fair to all users? Policies that fall within legal bounds can be determined to be illegal if they deny appropriate access to resources or impose unreasonable penalties on citizens.
3. Non-discriminatory Application: All policies should be applied fairly and equally to all library users. If the policies discriminate against certain types or groups of citizens, their legality can be called into question.
4. Measurability: Policies regarding users should be clearly written and displayed so those users will know what constitutes an infraction of policy. Policies should also be quantifiable so that breaches of policy can be fairly determined by information professionals and users.

NOTES

1. "Four Tests for a Legally Enforceable Library Policy." *Library of Michigan Access* 12 (September-October 1994): 9.

Chapter 2

How to Develop Policies

DETERMINING WHEN TO DEVELOP POLICIES

Policy development involves decisions to create, revise, or delete policies in order to stay current with changes in the library, its environment, and the needs of its staff and client groups.

New policy is developed to deal with recurring problems or situations. Generally, if a problem has arisen three or more times and been resolved each time on an ad hoc basis, there may be a need for a policy that will allow the situation to be resolved consistently in the future. For example, if serious complaints are repeatedly made about the way certain employees dress, there may be a need for a dress code. New policy can also be developed to anticipate problems that are expected to occur, such as user access conflicts that may arise when new electronic technologies are introduced.

Revision is the ongoing process of modifying and updating policies to accommodate significant changes—internal or external—to the library. Collection development policy might need to be revised if, for example, a large acquisition shifts the balance of the collection as a whole or if schools served by the public library close their libraries. Avoid the temptation, or pressure, to revise a policy based on conflict or crisis. Having a set schedule for examining policies allows time for tempers to cool and permits revisions to be discussed based on issues, and in the best interests of the patrons and community served.

Deletion is the removal of obsolete policies. These may include policies for programs or services, such as circulation of art prints or mail delivery of books, which have been discontinued. Many organizations retain outdated and obsolete policies, taking a laissez-faire approach that may lead to disillusionment on the part of those who must interpret and enforce policy. Further, if a library simply has too many policies or rules—whether outdated or current—it may develop a reputation for being overly rigid or unnecessarily bureaucratic.

Achieving an appropriate number and balance of useful policies requires informed judgment. Libraries should adopt policies that relate uniquely to their own roles, collections, services, and users. Each policy should be adopted for justifiable reasons, and these reasons should be known, understood, and explained to staff and patrons. The approach to policy enforcement should be flexible enough to allow for an exception—instead of policy revision—to be made when a genuine and understandable reason exists, or when an unfortunate precedent is not likely to be set. Check that the policy supports the primary and secondary roles of the library or in some way furthers the mission of the library.

Decisions on policy development should be made at least once a year during a review of all policies by library staff, the administration, and the board. This is the time to note if new policies are needed and which existing policies should be updated or deleted. A written administrative statement should mandate an annual review of policies by the governing authority. Review library policies, determine the work to be done, and establish a schedule for dealing with the development of new policy or the revision of existing ones on a logical basis throughout the year. Do not try to develop several new policies at the same time! Time is needed for research, consideration of the issues, discussion, and thought. Minor revisions to established policies, of course, will not require as much time as the development of new ones or major rewriting of outdated policies.

DEVELOPING EFFECTIVE POLICIES

Careful thought, discussion, and coordination are necessary for developing policies that will best serve the organization. To be effective, policies should be:

- Reflective of the mission, roles, and objectives of the organization. Individual policies should dovetail so that they build on each other.
- Consistent, in order to maintain efficiency. Contradictory policies counteract management goals.
- Flexible, to allow for some latitude in interpretation. Content should be assessed and updated regularly.
- Supported by procedures and rules. Procedures and rules are firm guides to action, exercising control and authority, whereas policies are flexible guides to thinking.
- Clearly written, so they are easily communicated to staff and users. A well-organized policy manual is a valuable aid to policy dissemination and use.

STEPS IN POLICY DEVELOPMENT

It might be helpful to think of the life cycle on page 12 for library policies.[1]

Policy statements are usually prepared, if not originated, by library staff. Although a board member or citizen may initiate the process, staff tends to be the first to recognize a situation that should be addressed by new policy. Staff and administrators develop and approve a proposed policy and present it to the library board or other governing authority for final approval. Board members are obligated to know good library practice, which will help them react to policy statements, challenge staff assumptions, and mold a policy that meets the needs of the library and the public. They may also be called upon to defend and support the policy if a citizen challenges it.

Step 1: Research. Policy makers should consider the philosophy behind and situation leading to the call for policy development. They should examine relevant documents such as the library's existing mission statement, documentation of the roles the library has selected for providing service, policies, procedures, rules, and regulations as well as relevant external laws and policies. They should be aware of any constraints relating to the library's budget, staffing, resources, services, and patrons. While it may be helpful to examine similar policies developed by other libraries, remember that your library is unique and you should not simply adapt the policies of another library to fit yours.

The Life Cycle of Library Policy

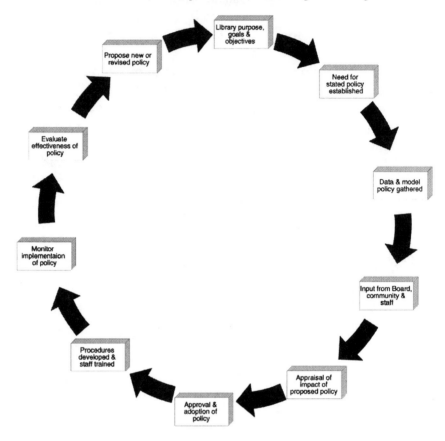

Step 2: Writing. Because policy statements must be understandable to a range of readers, including patrons, the text must be clear, brief, as free of professional jargon as possible, and carefully edited for spelling and grammar. The policy should be as brief as possible—no longer than one or two pages whenever possible—in a format consistent with the other policies of the library. Several drafts will probably be necessary in order to create a satisfactory "first draft" for review.

Step 3: Library Review. Depending on the library's size and organizational structure, the proposed policy may be reviewed in one or more meetings at one or more levels. At some point, it should be reviewed by the staff as a whole, the library director, and citizen representatives or groups such as Friends of the Library. Copies should be distributed a few days in advance of a meeting so that reviewers have time to read and consider the draft. If consensus cannot be reached during initial discussions, further meetings will have to be scheduled. Make note of policies or sections of policies that are mandated (either by local, state, or federal law or otherwise externally imposed), and, therefore, not part of the standard decision-making process. Groups working with the library to develop externally imposed policies will have less input and consensus may not be achievable.

Step 4: Revision. The text must be rewritten as many times as necessary to reflect the consensus.

Step 5: Library Approval. The revised version may be approved during a meeting or simply circulated for individual staff members to initial. If the library has an advisory board, rather than a governing board, approval from that group should be sought before submitting the policy to the governing authority for final adoption.

Step 6: Approval by Governing Authority. The proposed policy should be scheduled for presentation at the library board, city council, or commissioner's court meeting, and copies of the policy distributed a few days prior to the meeting. The policy will be presented, discussed, and possibly revised further. At the time of approval, it should be signed and dated by authorized representatives of the governing authority.

Step 7: Distribution. The approved policy should be distributed to each member of the board, administration, and staff and be added to the library's comprehensive policy manual. It should also be distributed and explained to new staff and patrons whenever appropriate.[2]

Step 8: Periodic Review. An annual review of all library policies will ensure the addition of new policies or the deletion of outdated or superfluous policies. Remember that policies are not carved in stone.[3] As your community changes and as the library's roles, goals, and resources change, policies must be reviewed and revised to reflect the current situations. Changes to existing policies will go through the same steps as new policy development described above.

POLICY MANUALS AND DISTRIBUTION

Because they are the primary vehicles for communicating policies to a variety of library personnel and patrons, policy manuals should be compiled, organized, and formatted for optimal readability and usability. Policy manuals should be easily accessible to staff, patrons, and any others who are affected by the policies. Keep in mind that the Americans with Disabilities Act also requires that policies be made available in alternate formats to be accessible to people with disabilities. Consider having the policy manual printed in large print and be prepared to have Braille and recorded versions available within a reasonable period of time if requested.

In addition to the types of policies in this book, a policy manual should contain the library's mission statement, a statement about the primary and secondary roles selected for library service, and important supporting documents, such as the American Library Association's *Library Bill of Rights*. The entire set of policies should be organized for easy access to a specific statement and should include an index, if possible, and a table of contents. Policies should be formatted and numbered consistently throughout, with dates of adoption and revision noted on each policy. Each policy should be approved and signed by the library's governing authority.

The format of the policy manual should facilitate updating and distribution. Many libraries compile policies in a loose-leaf notebook so that updated pages can be replaced individually and so specific policies can be reproduced and distributed as needed. While it might be useful to have a summary of important policies available as a brochure, copies of the entire manual should generally not be printed for public distribution because parts of the manual may soon be obsolete. Copies should be readily available for study by the public and copies of regularly needed policies may be printed for distribution. For example, the meeting room policy should be distributed with all applications to use the meeting room. Policies can also be distributed within an organization through letters, memoranda, and announcements, and posted on walls and bulletin boards for staff and patrons.

HOW TO USE MODEL POLICIES

This book offers models of most of the types of policies that will be useful in running a small- or medium-sized public library. Larger libraries, of course, also need most of these same policies, but may need others or may require policies that are more detailed. It is important to remember that a model policy does not fit every library. Although they can borrow and share ideas with other libraries, library staff should not simply copy the policy of another library. It is important that issues and options be discussed by the local people—staff, administrators, governing authority, advisory groups, and the public—who will have to apply, support, and defend the policies. The proper wording of a policy will vary depending upon the type of political structure that governs the library. Use these model policies, and any samples borrowed from other libraries, strictly as models. Always check with legal counsel and the governing authority for local style and proper language

NOTES

1. Curry, Betsy. *Georgia Public Library Trustees Handbook.* Georgia Library Trustee and Friends Association, 1984, p. 46.
2. Karpisek, Marian. "Policy Writing," in *Policymaking for School Library Media Programs*. Chicago: American Library Association, 1989, pp. 16-20.
3. Curry, Betsy. *Georgia Public Library Trustees Handbook.* Georgia Library Trustee and Friends Association, 1984, p. 46.

Chapter 3

Personnel and Employment Practices

Most public libraries operate as a department of a larger governmental body (city, municipality, county) that sets personnel policies affecting working conditions of all who are employed or who seek employment with that parent institution. If personnel functions are handled centrally, library staff members who interview potential candidates, make hiring decisions, or who evaluate and supervise staff must be familiar with established personnel guidelines. For such cases, the library may wish to have a general written policy that states that the library will conform to all governmentally established employment policies. If the library operates an independent personnel office or is an autonomous agency, it is even more critical that all appropriate personnel policies be in place. Libraries that are organized and run by a foundation or are owned by a private federated club should consult additional sources, including Chapter 4 of *Library and Information Center Management* by Robert Stueart and Barbara Moran, for detailed information on staffing.

It is important to have personnel policies readily and easily available to all who may be affected by them. These policies may protect the library from situations that encourage or permit nepotism and favoritism. It is also helpful to include a statement of governance (what body governs library personnel issues) and an organizational chart that shows the chain of command.

MODEL POLICY: PERSONNEL AND EMPLOYMENT PRACTICES

The (name of library) is a department of (city, county, municipality). Personnel services are coordinated through the (city, county, municipality) personnel office. The (name of library) supports and adheres to all laws and policies dealing with equal employment opportunity, the Civil Rights Acts, the Americans with Disabilities Act, fair employment practices, and other federal, state, and local legislation concerned with employment and hiring practices. Additional policies pertaining to library personnel practices have been implemented and are included in this policy manual.

Approved by (governing body) on (insert date)

_____

Signature of responsible representative

RECRUITMENT OF CANDIDATES FOR POSITIONS

Background

Workforce diversity is not only about being fair and equitable, it is also desirable. Persons from all segments of the community must be welcome to apply for positions with the library. In order to ensure equal opportunity, federal and state laws mandate that certain procedures and policies are in place so that all qualified candidates for employment will be treated fairly and equitably. Some cities, counties, or library districts are also subject to local civil service requirements. Diversity, and equitable access to jobs, begins with accurate, up-to-date job descriptions and the recruiting process. Julie B. Todaro's *A Practical Guide for Personnel Management: The Essential Elements* offers suggestions for selecting personnel, including advertising and job ad components, developing interview questions, and the selection process.

The Americans with Disabilities Act (ADA) covers the employment process, as well as access to the library's services. Job requirements must relate to the work expected and cannot require arbitrary physical abilities (such as height or weight restrictions). Job descriptions should be written to identify the essential functions of the job. Employers must also be prepared to provide reasonable accommodation to allow an otherwise qualified candidate with a disability to perform the job. Additional information on the employment process and the ADA can be found in Chapter 4 of *How Libraries Must Comply with the Americans with Disabilities Act (ADA)* by Donald D. Foos and Nancy C. Pack. The Job Accommodation Network (JAN) provides free information (call 800-526-7234) and consulting services about the employability of people with disabilities and job accommodation, as well as information regarding the Americans with Disabilities Act. Their Web site at http://janweb.icdi.wvu.edu/ provides links to the law and other documents related to ADA plus a variety of other resources. JAN also provides assistance to employers seeking ways to accommodate employees with disabilities, with more than 80% of the accommodations costing less than $500.

Issues

Are you aware of and familiar with *current* state and federal guidelines and regulations concerning employment practices?

Is the library responsible for recruitment or does the responsibility lie within a central personnel office? If recruitment is not the responsibility of the library, library administration can still assist the personnel department by suggesting the best places to reach qualified minority applicants. Many personnel departments will not be familiar with specialized library journals, electronic resources, and associations.

Are funds budgeted to advertise positions widely? When advertising positions, do you know how to reach qualified minority candidates? Many specialized journals, periodicals, and joblines exist. Do ads include a statement indicating that your library adheres to all Equal Employment Opportunity guidelines and encourages members of minority groups and people with disabilities to apply?

Have positions been identified where national searches are appropriate? Are funds available to help pay travel costs for qualified candidates who might not otherwise be able to travel to an interview? Have you considered alternative ways to interview (via conference call or at national or state conferences, for example) which might attract a more diverse group of candidates for positions?

Are job descriptions current? Do position requirements relate directly to the tasks required by the job and as described by the job description? Have job descriptions been updated to include essential physical requirements and are you prepared to make reasonable accommodation for job applicants as required by the Americans with Disabilities Act?

MODEL POLICY: RECRUITMENT OF CANDIDATES FOR POSITIONS

The (name of library) is committed to developing a diverse workforce. In hiring new staff and promoting current staff, the library will systematically and aggressively make reasonable effort to provide equal opportunity for all employees and applicants. An applicant pool that is representative of the makeup of the community is desirable. Positions will be advertised as widely as appropriate for the position and, when possible, advertising will be targeted to reach qualified candidates from minority groups and persons with disabilities. Reasonable accommodation will be made in accordance with the Americans with Disabilities Act for applicants and potential applications.

Approved by (governing body) on (insert date)

Signature of responsible representative

NEPOTISM

Background

Nepotism is hiring relatives to work in the same institution or the same work area. Employment policies should include a policy that clearly delineates when relatives cannot be hired and under what circumstance people who are related can work for the same organization (see model policy on page 22). Within the library, it would be inadvisable to have relatives working within the same range of supervision (reporting to the same supervisor). It would be unacceptable to have someone supervise his or her own relative. Larger organizations may be able to compartmentalize people who are related into different work areas, but this is less practical or attainable in smaller libraries. The policy statement should also address how the library will deal with changes in status following employment. For example, how will the library deal with two people who marry or become related through the marriage of other relatives?

Generally, relatives can be hired to work in another department of the same governing agency (for example, the sibling of someone working for the library could be hired by the city water department). It is prudent, however, to have a policy that addresses how relatives will be treated during the job recruitment process. This protects the library from being forced to hire the mayor's grandchild or the spouse of the police chief.

Issues

Do state nepotism laws exist that affect the library? Does the library's governing organization have policies that deal with relatives working in the same department or work program?

How large is your organization? Can the organizational structure accommodate people from the same family working under different chains of command?

How will you define "relatives"? Obvious relatives include spouse, children, parents, and siblings. What about aunts and uncles, grandparents, first cousins, and half-siblings or stepsiblings? Does the definition apply to the relatives of my spouse (for example, if I work for the library, could my husband's sister get a job there?)?

Will persons residing in the same household, but not related through blood or marriage, be treated as if they were related? Today people may share living quarters with and without personal attachments. Consider carefully the privacy issues that relate to living arrangements. Weigh the impact of becoming too involved in someone's personal life against the need of the library to avoid even the appearance of nepotism.

MODEL POLICY: NEPOTISM

The (name of library) will not hire the relatives of current employees. A relative is defined as the spouse, children, parents, grandparents, grandchildren, siblings, or aunts and uncles. Two persons residing in the same household who present themselves to the community as "a family" may not be employed by the library at the same time although they may not be legally related. Relatives of employees working in other city departments are not given special consideration in employment. Relatives will be considered for positions if they meet the job qualifications; an employee's relative may be hired if he or she is the best candidate for the position.

Approved by (governing body) on (insert date)

_____

Signature of responsible representative

STAFF DEVELOPMENT

Background

It is important that all staff, at every level of employment (including volunteers), be provided with initial and ongoing training to improve job performance and gain new skills. Staff should be encouraged to renew and expand their skills through cross-training, continuing education, and specialized training. Policies regarding release time from work, paid time for training, and reimbursement of training and education costs help ensure that all staff understand the nature and extent of available support.

Membership and involvement in professional associations is another form of staff development. Staff should be encouraged to join and participate in these organizations even if budget limitations or local governmental policies do not allow dues and registration fees to be paid from the library budget. Of course, whenever possible, paid time and financial support will encourage even more participation.

Some states have certification requirements that mandate continuing education for library staff. Many governing bodies require continuing education and development of new skills as a factor in the evaluation process, including allocation of merit increases and consideration for advancement or promotion. Knowledge of these requirements and their inclusion in a written policy, job descriptions, and performance evaluations helps to ensure that funds are budgeted for travel, fees, substitute staff, and materials. *Performance Analysis and Appraisal* by Robert D. Stueart and Maureen Sullivan includes additional information on staff development plans and their use in the evaluation of employee performance.

Issues

Does the library's governing authority have an overall orientation for new hires? Does the library have an orientation that introduces its policies, performance evaluation, chain of command, etc.? How will staff be oriented to the job for which they have been hired?

Is any library staff member subject to state or local certification or continuing education requirements? Do you know the timeline for meeting any mandated continuing education requirements? Are continuing education, professional association involvement, and other training included in job requirements? Be sure to distinguish between staff development and required job training, which must take priority. For example, state law may require that the administrative assistant take a state-provided course in records management in order to ensure that appropriate records of government decisions are kept for the appropriate period of time.

What are the potential sources for training and continuing education? What training and staff development opportunities are provided by the library's governing body? How far will staff have to travel to obtain training? What costs are associated with receiving training? What non-library specific training is available locally and regionally (for example, computer training, management skills, foreign language)? Do you know if other training materials, such as books, videotapes, etc., are available, and are funds budgeted to rent or purchase items if they cannot be borrowed?

Is personal development included in job performance evaluations and/or a factor in receiving salary increases, merit raises, and promotions? Are sample staff development plans available for individuals to review?

Does the library's governing authority have a policy regarding release time for training? Are restrictions placed on travel (e.g., permission is required to leave the county; no out-of-state travel; limited reimbursement, etc.)?

Are substitutes available to cover service desks while staff is away? Staff size, availability of substitutes, and other staffing considerations may preclude training that requires extensive travel or extended time away from the library. If this is the case, what alternatives are available?

Will the library support involvement in professional associations by encouraging membership and providing financial support for involvement in association activities? Do local laws and policies permit the library to reimburse all or part of association dues? Do local laws and policies permit, encourage, or specifically prohibit the use of staff time for association activities and for staff to hold office in associations? Are there other organizations and associations that, while not library specific, relate to the library's mission and roles (for example, local business clubs, the Chamber of Commerce, International Reading Association, or the National Association for the Education of Young People)? Will the library support membership in those organizations?

PERFORMANCE EVALUATION AND SALARY INCREASES

Background

Ways in which salaries are determined, how employee performance is evaluated and the impact of performance on salaries, and decisions about when and how salaries will be increased or decreased must be established in advance and be available for review by all who are affected by these policies. Knowing how salaries are set and under what conditions raises will be awarded is vital to staff morale. Everyone has the right to know how their job performance will be evaluated, when written evaluations will take place, and to have, as much as possible, objective and measurable goals against which their performance will be measured. Detailed assistance on writing effective job descriptions, developing performance plans, and staff performance review methods and processes is available in *Performance Analysis and Appraisal* by Robert D. Stueart and Maureen Sullivan.

MODEL POLICY: STAFF DEVELOPMENT

The (name of library) is committed to having a trained and educated workforce. During the first week on the job, every new employee will receive a general orientation to the library. During that time, the employee and his or her supervisor will develop an individualized training timeline based on the job requirements, experience, and educational needs for the particular position.

Basic dues for the state professional association will be reimbursed, funds permitting, for all permanent, full-time staff members (including paraprofessional and clerical staff who join appropriate organizations). If funds are not available to cover the entire cost of basic dues, each employee will receive a prorated share of available funds. The library director may also approve financial and other support for staff to join non-library-related organizations that further the library's roles (for example, the Chamber of Commerce or International Reading Association).

Every staff member is encouraged to have a written staff development plan prepared in consultation with his or her supervisor. All staff members are encouraged to attend job-related workshops and seminars to fulfill their staff development plan. Three workdays (24 hours) of work release time is available annually for each full-time employee to attend optional job-related training and educational functions. Part-time employees will receive prorated release time. Funds will be budgeted as equitably as possible to cover the travel expenses and registration fees for this training.

Additional work time may be given to attend training that meets the employee's staff development plan. Travel expenses and registration fees will be reimbursed if funds are available, upon approval of the library director.

Professional and paraprofessional staff are encouraged to attend library science and related professional association meetings, such as the ALA annual conference, state library association conferences, and regional conferences. Funds are budgeted for this purpose and staff wishing to attend conferences should indicate their interest to the library director early in the budget year. If there are not sufficient funds to cover costs for all employees wishing to attend conferences, funds will be given first towards the expenses of staff members who have official responsibilities or who are officers of the association. Remaining funds will be prorated so that as many staff members as possible have some financial support. Attendance at professional association conferences and meetings will be rotated as equitably as possible among staff members.

Professional staff is expected to stay familiar with current issues in librarianship by reading professional journals and library literature. Funds are budgeted to purchase the major professional journals and books. Requests that the library purchase specific books, periodicals, videos, audiotapes, and other materials specifically for staff development should be made to the library director (or other designated staff member). Funds are budgeted to purchase items that will be useful to more than one staff member. In some cases, videos, films, and audiotapes may be borrowed or rented for limited use.

In order that training may be shared with other staff, written reports will be required within five workdays of an employee's return from training. Employees may also be required to conduct programs, seminars, and similar activities for other staff. When necessary, one-on-one training between staff may also be required.

Approved by (governing body) on (insert date)

_____
Signature of responsible representative

Issues

Who is authorized to set salaries? Are salary ranges set for each position? Who can authorize hiring at a salary above entry level and what factors (education, experience, previous salary, difficulty in filling the position) permit hiring above entry level? Are unions, employee organizations, or other legal authorities involved in establishing salaries?

Does the library or parent organization have an established process to evaluate job performance? How frequently are written evaluations performed? Are salary increases tied to periodic performance evaluations? If job performance is satisfactory, are salary increases automatic? Is there a probationary period for new employees?

Under what circumstances can an employee receive a salary increase greater than one step on the salary scale? What happens when an employee "tops out" on the pay scale?

Are funds available for longevity pay, merit bonuses, or extra pay for specific abilities (bilingual proficiency, for example), working outside of normal business hours (Sunday pay after 40 hours), hazardous work (emergency conditions), or premium work (being subject to call back during off time)? How is overtime pay handled? Are some employees exempt from overtime pay, subject to flat rate pay, or given compensatory time instead of overtime pay? Is compensatory time awarded at a rate other than one hour for each hour worked? Are you familiar with federal Fair Labor Standards Act rules and do you know which staff positions may be subject to them?

Are all employees subject to the same salary scales, provisions for salary increases, etc., regardless of the source of funds for their salary? Are there positions that are funded from sources other than the library's regular funding source (such as grants or temporary positions) that are exempt from the policies that govern pay increases, longevity pay, merit increases, etc.?

EMPLOYEE BENEFITS

Background

Employee benefits generate the next largest budget item, after salaries, for most libraries. Benefits can often be as important to employees as salary level. Every employee should be aware of all benefits available and know how to receive them. If benefits are different for part-time or temporary employees, or for someone in a position that is funded from sources such as grant money, these deviations from standard policy should be clearly identified. If the library is part of a larger governmental body, benefits are usually uniform for all departments of that governmental body.

Issues

What benefits are offered by the library's governing authority? Are optional benefits available (dependent health insurance, disability insurance) or are some benefits available as "menu" selections from which employees can choose?

If the library is a department of a larger governmental body, what flexibility, if any, is accorded individual departments in ad-

MODEL POLICY:
PERFORMANCE EVALUATIONS AND SALARY INCREASES

Salary ranges are established for each position classification by the (governing authority) and are posted in the personnel office and the staff lounge. New employees are generally hired at the base level of the salary range. When approved by the library director, new hires may enter at a higher salary range based on exceptional experience, education, or other appropriate factors.

Within one month of employment, a job performance plan will be established for each employee and a written copy given to the employee. The first job performance evaluation will be conducted at the end of a six-month probationary period. Performance plans will be set and evaluations will be scheduled for a period of one year unless circumstances warrant a shorter period for the review.

Upon completion of a satisfactory performance evaluation, an employee will be considered for a merit raise. Merit raises are awarded only once in a year even if more than one performance evaluation is completed during that time.

Longevity pay, annual merit bonuses, and cost-of-living increases are established by (governing authority) and are generally given across the board to all employees who meet the established criteria.

The (name of library) expects that staff will be able to perform required work within a forty-hour workweek. When staff is required to work overtime, with approval of the library director or in emergency situations, compensatory time will be awarded for actual time worked. The (name of library) does not budget for overtime pay, which will be paid only under extenuating circumstances when authorized by the library director and approved by the (governing authority).

Approved by (governing body) on (insert date)

_____
Signature of responsible representative

ministering the overriding policies? For example, can the library require that vacation requests be submitted a specific period of time in advance? Having the ability to require sufficient advance notice of vacation can be critical to ensuring that adequate staff remains to cover service desks.

How are sick leave and vacation leave accrued? Under what circumstances are employees able to use these types of leave? Are other types of leave available (jury duty, bereavement leave, leave without pay); how are they defined and under what circumstances may these types of leave be used?

Are there other types of benefits available, such as child care or elder care supplements, car-pooling subsidies, free parking, tuition reimbursement, and service awards?

MODEL POLICY: EMPLOYEE BENEFITS

Benefits such as health insurance, group insurance, vacation and sick leave, paid time off, employee retirement plans, child care or elder care supplements, car-pool subsidies, and other miscellaneous benefits (travel expenses, tuition reimbursements, access to subsidized day care, etc.) are established and administered by (name of governing authority). The (name of library) may not increase or decrease these benefits without written authorization from (governing authority).

Requests for vacation leave must be submitted to the library director in writing at least two weeks before the date that leave will begin. Effort will be made to accommodate leave requests during holiday periods but staffing needs may preclude approval of all requests. Sick leave may be used for doctor appointments, but, to ensure adequate staffing, must be submitted at least one week in advance except in emergencies. Sick leave may not be claimed while on vacation leave. A maximum of three days each year may be granted for other types of leave (bereavement or other emergency leave) upon approval of the library director.

Approved by (governing body) on (insert date)

_____

Signature of responsible representative

USE OF VOLUNTEERS

Background

Volunteers can add immensely to the quality of service that the library can provide. Volunteers act as public relations spokespersons for the library, becoming "friends" of the library. A volunteer program also offers a means for members of the community to give of themselves and give back to their community. Volunteers should be used to provide specific and selective services and should not replace permanent, paid staff. It is important to remember that volunteers are not "free," they require training, supervision, development, and encouragement. The best volunteers will take their job just as seriously as paid staff does, but permanent staff will spend varying amounts of time recruiting volunteers, training them, and supervising their work.

Issues

Have you identified the ways in which volunteers could contribute to the library and its services? Do union rules, local laws, and the policies of the library's governing authority permit the use of volunteers?

Do you have a process for reporting volunteer time? Have you considered ways to avoid any negative effect on the budget from using volunteers? Volunteers should supplement, not supplant, permanent paid staff.

Who will recruit, train, and monitor volunteers? Job descriptions must be available for all volunteer positions. Potential volunteers must be interviewed, selected, and trained for positions in much the same way as paid staff. Volunteers have a lot to offer libraries, but need the same supervision and guidance as paid staff.

Will those who have volunteered be considered when paying positions are available? Some libraries avoid hurt feelings or problems with favoritism by stating up front that volunteers will not be considered for paid employment. Other libraries look at volunteers as a valuable pool of potential applicants who already have some job training and familiarity with the organization. Regardless of potential future employment, all volunteers need to have their work recognized.

Will children and teenagers be used as volunteers? Young people can provide great enthusiasm and energy, but volunteering should not be a substitute for child care or summer camp. Youth volunteers usually require closer supervision, continued motivation, and more social interaction. Do child labor laws limit the number of hours or restrict the times a young person can work and do those laws apply for non-paid work? A parental permission form and disclaimer of liability is highly recommended for youth volunteers.

Are community service restitution "volunteers" to be used? These are people required by a court or other law enforcement agency to perform community service. These "volunteers" may be very motivated to provide short-term, intensive services.

Can staff volunteer in any capacity? Fair labor laws or the policies of the library's governing entity may prohibit a staff member from volunteering to perform any activity for which they would normally be paid. However, staff may be able to volunteer in areas

MODEL POLICY: USE OF VOLUNTEERS

The (name of library) welcomes and encourages members of the community to volunteer their time and talents to enrich and expand library services. Volunteers are expected to conform to all policies of (name of library) and the rules outlined in the volunteer handbook, and are selected and retained for as long as the library needs their services. Volunteers may be used for special events, projects, and activities or on a regular basis to assist staff. Services provided by volunteers will supplement, but not replace, regular services, and volunteers will not be used in place of hiring full- or part-time staff. Volunteers may apply for paid positions under the same conditions as other outside applicants. In accordance with labor laws and the policies of (governing entity), paid staff may not volunteer their services to the library except with written permission from the library director. Staff may volunteer in other departments of city government outside the library.

Approved by (governing body) on (insert date)

———————————————————————————————
Signature of responsible representative

outside their normal duties or in other departments of city or county service.

TERMINATION OF EMPLOYMENT

Background

People leave their jobs for a variety of reasons, sometimes voluntarily and other times due to termination through firing or layoffs. Employees who resign to take another job can be a valuable source of information about what is not working right within your organization. To ensure a smooth transition of job responsibilities following a resignation, employees should be expected to provide reasonable notice and to do what they can to complete unfinished projects or transfer responsibility to another staff member. Those following the established procedures for resignation may be entitled to specific benefits.

Budget cuts may require that some employees are laid off and policies will establish what benefits they may be entitled to as part of the layoff. Employees who are fired may be entitled to a grievance process or other rights.

Policies make clear how terminations will be handled under the various situations and make the process of leaving equitable and more pleasant for everyone. General policies, which must be adhered to by all departments, may be established by the library's governing authority.

Issues

If an employee is leaving for another job, how far in advance must notice be given? Reasonable notice may differ for specific positions depending upon the complexities of the job and staffing levels. For example, it might be reasonable to ask for three weeks' notice for professional level positions, but only one week for shelver and aide positions. Is less notice required if the employee is transferring to another division or department of the same governing authority? If reasonable notice is not given, are some benefits denied? What benefits must be accorded by law (vacation pay, continued insurance coverage)?

MODEL POLICY: TERMINATION OF EMPLOYMENT

Employees who resign to accept employment with another business or to leave the workforce must give two weeks' written notice in order to leave in good standing. Employees who leave in good standing will be paid for unused vacation and compensatory time on their final paycheck and will be eligible for rehire in the future. An exit interview will be scheduled with the library director on the last day of employment. All library property, including keys and identification cards, must be returned before issuance of the final paycheck.

Employees may be terminated for substandard work without notice during the probationary period. After the probation period, employees will receive oral and written counseling to improve substandard work before dismissal if work does not improve. Serious offenses, such as theft, use of drugs or alcohol while at work, and physical assault, may result in immediate dismissal without counseling. Employees who are terminated may file a grievance with (governing authority) within five days of termination. A grievance appeal must be made in writing.

If budget cuts necessitate a reduction in staffing levels, the library director will determine which positions can be cut to create the least overall negative effect on library services. The director's plan will be submitted to (governing authority) for approval before implementation. Longevity will be a primary factor in retaining staff, and whenever possible, staff will be moved into vacant positions for which they are qualified. Employees who are laid off will be paid for all unused vacation, compensatory time, and sick leave.

Approved by (governing body) on (insert date)

———————————————————————————
Signature of responsible representative

What conditions must exist for an employee to be dismissed? Know the policies of the library's governing authority and any procedures that must be followed. Are there actions (such as theft, misuse of funds, time, or library resources, excessive absence, harassment) that can lead to immediate dismissal?

If budget cuts require a reduction in the workforce, how will decisions be made as to which positions will be cut? What rights and benefits are accorded those who are laid off? What outplacement resources are available within the organization and the community to aid the employee's transition?

Do union rules, or agreements with employee groups, affect policies about terminations? Are any positions designated as serving at the pleasure of the director or another official? Are hourly employees subject to different rules than salaried staff? Are grievance procedures in place for employees to contest decisions about layoff or firing?

Chapter 4

Staff Conduct

The staff is the greatest asset of the library; without them the books, materials, and building are of little value. Staff has an obligation to maintain a high standard of ethical behavior. Because of their position with the library, some privileges may be available to them that are not afforded the public. Policies dealing with staff conduct and behavior ensure that every staff member knows the parameters and is aware that breach of conduct will be dealt with in a fair and consistent manner.

Additionally, staff dress, demeanor, and conduct set the tone for library patrons. If the library is to be seen as a friendly, open, business-like agency, staff must adhere to guidelines for conduct. Guidelines for conduct also help to create an environment conducive to quality job performance and provide opportunities for each staff member to know what is expected of him or her.

CODE OF ETHICS

Background

Ethics are the principles of conduct and the moral values that govern the actions of an individual or a group. In public service organizations, honesty and integrity are the cornerstones of trust. For librarians and library staff, the American Library Association has established a code of ethics, revised in 1995. Additionally, some state library associations have either endorsed the American Library Association code or supplemented it with one of their own. Some state and local governmental bodies also establish codes of ethics for public employees.

Although library trustees are included in the American Library Association Code of Ethics, they have also recognized their ethical obligations and established their own code of ethics, which is set forth in *Public Libraries*.[1] Other groups, such as the Association for Library Collections & Technical Services (ALCTS) have also adopted supplemental ethics statements that focus more directly to their area of concern.[2]

Issues

Public employees are held to a high standard of conduct. The American Library Association Code of Ethics establishes high expectations for the profession. Public authority cannot enforce ethical guidelines, although sometimes local policies and regulations may afford penalties for specific violations. For example, the Code of Ethics stipulates that librarians must protect each user's right to privacy; most states now have laws mandating the confidentiality of patron records and affording penalties for violating that privacy. Do you know what laws in your community might relate to or enforce the ALA Code of Ethics or state library association statements on ethics?

Agree on a working definition of ethics. Richard Rubin recommends the following definition: "Ethical considerations are those involved in deciding what is good or right in terms of the treatment of human beings, human actions and values. It involves determining what people 'ought' to do, in distinction from what individuals may be forced to do, as in when one is legally required to act in a certain way."[3]

Adherence to a code of ethics sets a professional apart from someone who is just doing a job. Do you agree that every library staff member, regardless of his or her educational degrees, salary, or position is a library professional?

Discuss how the tenets of the American Library Association Code of Ethics or statements on ethics by the state library association or other organizations will help the library director, board members, and staff understand the practical philosophy that sup-

MODEL POLICY: CODE OF ETHICS

The (name of library) endorses the American Library Association Code of Ethics and the (name of state library association) "Statement on Ethics" and expects that all staff will strive to maintain the highest levels of personal and professional integrity. Additionally, the trustees for (name of library) will follow the code of ethics established by the American Library Trustees Association (ALTA) in carrying out the duties and responsibilities of their office.

Public employees are held to a high standard of ethical behavior. No staff member may accept or solicit any gift or service that is offered to influence the employee's action, seeks to curry special privileges or favors, or is given to reward the employee for doing his or her job. Token items, such as food or flowers, may be accepted and shared with other staff. Items of value must be refused or returned to the giver. In exceptional cases where the item cannot be returned, the library director will donate the item to an appropriate local charity such as Goodwill.

Staff is also prohibited from using their position for private gain and from transacting library business with any entity in which they have a financial interest (see also policy on "Selling and Soliciting in the Library").

Staff will receive training and opportunities to discuss case studies in areas of librarianship that might present ethical dilemmas. Staff is encouraged to discuss any concerns about their own handling of potential problems with their supervisor or the library director before or after a situation has occurred.

Approved by (governing body) on (insert date)

Signature of responsible representative

ports the reasons for behaviors outlined in other policies. Our obligation is to the patron and service to the public. Endorsement of a code of ethics reminds us of this obligation and reinforces the organization's commitment to the highest quality of service and ethical treatment of people.

Are there local ordinances related to conflict of interest, use of office for private gain, or rules related to acceptance of gifts by public employees? These rules, if applicable, or the concepts they regulate should also be incorporated into a policy on ethics.

Has staff received training in potential problem areas and do you have an ongoing process of continued discussion about situations that have or might present ethical problems?

DRESS CODE

Background

The way in which we dress sets the tone for many aspects of our work. While staff should be encouraged to dress for comfort and safety, some guidelines let staff know what is acceptable and what is discouraged or prohibited (see model policy on page 40). Style of dress is very personal and many people use the way they dress and the jewelry or accessories they wear to make a personal statement. The library director has no authority to mandate personal beliefs or regulate dress outside of the library, but the library is not an appropriate place to make personal statements that intentionally or deliberately offend or inflame the public who come into the library.

Issues

If the library is part of a larger governmental body, is there an overall dress code? Are you familiar with the prevailing business dress code for your community? Some areas of the country have dress codes that are more casual (in the South, for example, it is often acceptable for men to forgo ties during the summer). Smaller communities may view a casual style of dress as being "more friendly." Library staff should dress comfortably, but suitably for the position held and the type of work performed.

Standards should be tolerant to individual styles of dress, ethnic culture, and religious requirements. Staff with disabilities may also need to dress differently than one might expect for a business. Are you familiar with dress requirements for special situations? These situations may require leniency in style of dress but no situation should permit staff to dress in a sloppy or unclean manner.

Are you aware of current fashion trends that might temporarily change the way staff dresses? Are T-shirts acceptable attire for any staff? If so, may staff wear T-shirts that promote causes, cultural icons, or statements of belief? Are you familiar with current slang, including words in foreign languages, that may appear on T-shirts?

How tolerant is the community towards counterculture or alternative fashions, such as body piercing, tattoos, and unusual hair fashions? Jewelry can also create image problems if it is excessively flamboyant, consists of obscene or illegal images (such as body parts or drugs), or interferes with the staff member's ability to work. Staff can also be expected to dress appropriately for their gender (mores are more tolerant towards women in masculine attire than they are towards men dressing in skirts and dresses).

Personal hygiene can be a very touchy problem. A staff member who does not bathe frequently enough, has unclean hair, or uses excessive amounts of cologne creates an unpleasant and unprofessional environment. Heavy odors, even those that are pleasant in moderation, can also trigger allergies or physical illness in others. This managerial or supervisory problem must be dealt with tactfully. Keep in mind that some odors may be indicators of health problems and the staff member may not even realize that there is a problem.

Does the work in some job categories require or allow a more lenient dress code? Some libraries distinguish between staff seen by the public and those who are not, although in most small- and medium-sized libraries any staff member may be called into service to cover a public desk or meet with a citizen. Jobs that are typically filled by students or that require working in a messy environment often allow for more casual dress, but a dress code should mandate that casual does not mean sloppy, unsafe, or disruptive.

Are there times when leisure clothing or costume would be appropriate? Some libraries encourage staff to dress "western" for rodeo days, dress in costume for Halloween, or wear reading and library related T-shirts and jeans to kick off summer reading programs. Some libraries also designate Fridays as casual days, permitting staff to wear jeans or other casual attire. If casual or costume days are established, clothing should still be clean and appropriately modest (no belly dancer costumes or swimsuits!).

MODEL POLICY: DRESS CODE

Public image plays an important role in developing and maintaining support for the (name of library). In order to maintain a public image consistent with a professional organization, it is expected that each staff member's dress and grooming will be appropriate for a business environment and in keeping with his or her work assignment. Health and safety standards must also be considered in dressing for work.

Clothing and accessories must be neat and clean, and should not draw inappropriate or disruptive attention to the individual. Staff members working with the public should be dressed for a business setting. Staff members who shelve materials, work outdoors, or whose work is confined to the back office areas may dress more casually. Shorts, halter tops, and bare feet are never permitted. T-shirts or other attire that promote political causes, campaigns, or issues may not be worn. Obscenities, euphemisms, or slang words for foul language, and foreign phrases that could be interpreted inappropriately are also not permitted.

Staff working in public areas may not wear radio or cassette player headphones. Questions regarding appropriate attire or exceptions to the dress code must be directed to the library director.

Approved by (governing body) on (insert date)

_____

Signature of responsible representative

STAFF USE OF LIBRARY MATERIALS AND EQUIPMENT

Background

Staff has access to library materials and equipment to a greater degree than is afforded the public. This access brings with it a higher degree of responsibility. Staff must keep in mind that the needs of the community come first. They are not entitled to special privileges, such as lengthier check-out periods, due to their employment, although the library board or governing authority may wish to confer some degree of privilege.

MODEL POLICY:
STAFF USE OF LIBRARY MATERIALS AND EQUIPMENT

Staff must exercise extreme caution in the access and use of materials and equipment placed in their trust. Library materials or equipment for personal use must be checked out if they are to be removed from the library. Large quantities of material should not be held out of the collection for extended periods for staff use. Staff will not be charged for overdue fines or reserves, but will be subject to disciplinary action if materials are not returned and discharged before the system generates a second overdue notice. Staff will not be charged for reasonable use of library equipment but equipment must be reserved and properly checked out. Staff may not make personal copies on the photocopier using the bypass key. Violation of any part of this policy may be considered theft of property or services and subject to disciplinary or legal action.

Approved by (governing body) on (insert date)

_____

Signature of responsible representative

Issues

Is staff required to check out all materials for personal use outside of the library? Staff checkout adds to the circulation figures (library staff can also be library patrons) and maintains control over inventory. Additionally, requiring that all materials be checked out avoids allegations of theft.

Are fines forgiven for overdue materials checked out by staff? This can be a reasonable perquisite if it is not abused. What constitutes abuse of circulation periods and what action will take place if a staff members keeps material out for too long?

Is staff required to pay fees for personal use of equipment (such as projectors, cassette recorders, etc.) if fees are charged to patrons?

Will staff be permitted to make personal copies with the copier bypass key? Even if the copier does not have a per-copy cost associated with it, paper and toner are used and excessive staff copying depletes resources intended for the general public and for the daily operations of the library.

SELLING AND SOLICITING IN THE LIBRARY

Background

Staff and patrons have the right to work in or use the library without being subject to sales and solicitations by others. Selling and solicitation by patrons may be included in a policy dealing with distribution of materials in the library. Generally, it is best not to turn the library into a swap meet or bargaining floor.

Rules for interacting with other staff may be more lenient than are rules for interacting with patrons. Some staff may be prohibited, by the nature of their position, from having employment outside the library or from selling or buying items from the people under their supervision. In any case, appropriate selling or solicitation must be defined. Staff members who do not wish to avail themselves of offered items or services must be protected. Care must be exercised to avoid any suggestion of improper or undue pressure on employees to purchase items from their supervisor(s) or fellow employees.

Issues

Is there a staff lounge or other appropriate place for library employees to post announcements or solicitations? Are there local or state laws that govern staff interactions while on and off duty? Do policies of the library's governing authority regulate outside employment by any categories of staff?

Does the library's policy on "Use of Meeting Room" permit selling in the meeting room? If so, staff should apply for and use the meeting room as a private citizen under the same conditions stipulated for the public.

MODEL POLICY: SELLING AND SOLICITING IN THE LIBRARY

It is recognized that library employees may engage in the sale of goods or services outside of their employment with the library. It is never appropriate to solicit business from staff or patrons during library work time. Soliciting business from patrons during off-work time while on library property is not permitted; however, staff may offer their business card if requested. Information regarding personal business may be distributed to other employees by placing ads on the staff bulletin board, posting information regarding the business, off-work hours, and contact information, or by leaving catalogs or brochures in the staff room. Oral and/or written invitations to product parties, sending out of information through interoffice mail, or display of items for sale are not permitted on library property.

Approved by (governing body) on (insert date)

_____

Signature of responsible representative

POLITICAL ACTIVITIES BY EMPLOYEES

Background

Everyone has the right to hold political opinions and to promote his or her political beliefs. However, such activities should be limited to off-work time and may not be appropriately pursued while representing the library (see model policy on page 44). Staff and patrons should never be unwillingly subjected to proselytizing or lobbying by library employees.

Issues

Are there local ordinances or state laws governing political activity by public employees that would include library employees?

Are the library and its staff subject to rules from a union or bargaining group? Does the library have a policy on distribution of materials in the library? Does it permit the distribution or posting of political information? Staff may be entitled to distribute information, as private citizens, in the information center or on a bulletin board under the same conditions as the public.

MODEL POLICY: POLITICAL ACTIVITIES BY EMPLOYEES

Employees may engage in political activities on their own time. However, (jurisdictional authority) limits the employees' right to express their political opinion during work hours. Prohibited activities include but are not limited to wearing campaign or political buttons, distributing campaign or political literature, except as permitted in the library's policy on "Distribution of Free Materials," and expressing political opinions while on work time. T-shirts or other attire that promotes a particular political issue, person, or cause are not appropriate (see also "Dress Code"). Bumper stickers may not be applied to library property or library vehicles.

Approved by (governing body) on (insert date)

_____

Signature of responsible representative

DISCOUNTS ON STAFF BOOK PURCHASES

Because libraries can buy books and other materials at a substantial discount, some libraries permit staff to make personal purchases through the library account. Care must be taken to see that this privilege does not result in undue time spent placing orders and collecting from staff. Patrons and staff in other city or county departments may also feel that the library should order materials for them if this privilege is not structured carefully. If this is a service the library wants to provide for other city or county departments, policy should establish conditions to avoid any improper use of public funds and to minimize staff time used for personal purchases.

Issues

Do the policies of the library's governing authority permit personal items to be ordered through the library's vendor with payment being made by the staff member?

Does the library have a staff association? Often the staff association can establish its own account with a library vendor (Baker & Taylor or Ingram, for example) and association officers handle the orders and payment, removing the financial mechanics from the library's bill.

Does the library or staff association want to handle cash or must payment be made by check? Cash makes it harder to ensure proper credit and maintain a paper trail if problems arise.

Does the library wish to offer this perquisite to employees of other city or county departments? Will doing so create a burden for library staff or interfere with their ability to carry out their own work?

MODEL POLICY: DISCOUNTS ON STAFF BOOK PURCHASES

Library staff members may order books and other library materials for personal use at a discount through the staff association. Discounts cannot be guaranteed and books, once ordered, may not be returned unless received in damaged condition. Payment must be made, by check, within two workdays after the item is received. Abuse of this policy will result in loss of the privilege to purchase books through the library staff association. This privilege is limited to library staff and may be discontinued at any time at the discretion of the library director.

Approved by (governing body) on (insert date)

Signature of responsible representative

STAFF RELATIONS AND CELEBRATIONS

We frequently spend more time with our co-workers than we do with our families. Co-workers should be encouraged to enjoy each other as individuals, required to respect everyone's abilities, and expected to treat each other with dignity and fairness. Parties and celebrations can be a time to pull people together but, if not handled properly, these events can cause resentment and friction. No one should ever be required to participate in staff celebrations, contribute to gift funds, or in any way be coerced into socializing.

MODEL POLICY: STAFF RELATIONS AND CELEBRATIONS

Good staff relations and the development of a cohesive work team benefit from some socializing. Therefore, the (name of library) encourages a reasonable amount of socializing and staff celebration so long as these events do not interfere with the normal flow of work. Birthdays should be celebrated one time per month with all birthdays for that month recognized at the same time. Staff parties to celebrate holidays will be scheduled at times with minimal impact to service and all service desks must be covered during parties. Every staff member is welcome to attend any party held during work hours on library property. Parties scheduled outside of work time and off library property are considered personal parties but, in the interest of good staff relations, party planners are encouraged to include all staff members in the festivities.

Gifts between individual staff members are not prohibited, but group gifts should be given equitably. Solicitation for contributions for group gifts should be done anonymously by routing an envelope. Supervisors may not accept gifts, except for token, inexpensive items such as coffee mugs, pens, and candy, from the people they directly supervise.

Approved by (governing body) on (insert date)

_____

Signature of responsible representative

Issues

Does the library have a staff association that organizes celebrations and staff events? Does that group have written guidelines to ensure that every staff member is treated equally in social events?

Are there any policies or rules developed by the library's governing agency that restrict or prohibit recognition of birthdays, use of staff time or library funds for parties, etc.?

Can staff rooms and library meeting rooms be used for staff functions or must all socializing be done off library property?

Do you want to establish guidelines to reduce the number of parties and group functions? Depending on how large the staff (do not forget volunteers!) is, individual celebration of birthdays can get out of hand.

NOTES

1. "Ethics Statement for Public Library Trustees." *Public Libraries* 24, no. 4 (Winter 1985): 166.
2. "ALCTS Board of Directors approve ethics statement." Press release, American Library Association, April 1994.
3. Rubin, Richard. "Ethical Issues in Library Personnel Management." *Journal of Library Administration* 14, no. 4 (September 1991): 1–16.

Chapter 5

Access to Library Services

Libraries are more than collections of books and other materials in a building. The library provides services, which can range from public meeting places to assistance with homework. Policies that clearly explain what library services are available, under what conditions, and to whom, will go far toward ensuring fair and equitable access to everything the library can offer to everyone in the community. The library should also establish its primary roles, based on the Public Library Association's (PLA) *Planning & Role Setting for Public Libraries* or the updated service options that PLA released in 1998. The policy manual should include a mission statement that details those roles. A synopsis of the PLA roles is included in Appendix H of this book.

AMERICANS WITH DISABILITIES ACT

Background

The passage of Public Law 101-336, the Americans with Disabilities Act of 1990 (usually referred to as ADA), by the United States Congress in July 1990 was viewed by many as the "Emancipation Proclamation" for the millions of Americans who have one or more physical or mental disability. This comprehensive law requires changes in a variety of areas, including transportation, telecommunications, employment, and public accommodation.[1] Libraries must comply with the section of the Americans with Disabilities

Act dealing with public accommodation. (Employers, including libraries, must also have non-discriminatory job application procedures, qualification standards, selection criteria, and conditions of employment, but these issues are addressed in the employment policies of the library or by the governing body that oversees the personnel needs of the library (see model policy on page 52).) If you have not read the ADA, copies are available on the Internet through several sites, including the Job Accommodation Network. (http://janweb.icdi. wvu.edu)

All government facilities and all entities that serve the public must make their buildings and services accessible to persons with disabilities. Physical barriers should be removed and auxiliary aids and services must be provided to individuals with disabilities. Reasonable accommodation must be made to ensure that, whenever possible, persons with disabilities can use library services and gain access to public areas without assistance or intervention. If areas or services can not be made accessible, other methods to deliver the same service must be provided (for example, retrieving items stored on high shelves, providing library forms and documents in alternative formats, or relocating a program to an accessible area). Additional information on making library facilities and services accessible is available in *The Americans with Disabilities Act: Its Impact on Libraries* edited by Joanne L. Crispen. This resource includes a detailed self-evaluation survey. *The ADA Library Kit: Sample ADA-Related Documents to Help You Implement the Law*, edited by Kathleen Mayo and Ruth O'Donnell, offers sample community surveys, accommodation forms and notices, compliance plans, and staff training information.

The Americans with Disabilities Act provides the legal basis to end discrimination, and a policy supporting ADA demonstrates that the library is committed to providing access to its facilities and services. Training for staff and the inclusion of people with disabilities on library advisory committees, governing boards, and related citizen input groups will encourage lasting and real changes.

Issues

Have you read the Americans with Disabilities Act of 1990 and are you familiar with its requirements? Has the library completed an ADA self-evaluation, as required by the law, and is a compliance plan in place? Has the plan been updated and reviewed on a regular basis? Is there a procedure in place for persons with disabilities to request accommodation or provide input or complaints about services? (See also the policy on "Public Participation in Library Decision Making.")

Do you know what areas of the library building might pose problems for persons with disabilities? Have you examined ways to correct or adjust those problems or to offer the same service in a different, more accessible location in the library?

Have you included local agencies, organizations, and disability groups in the planning process? Do you have up-to-date contact information on those resources? Do you know how to locate sign language interpreters, Braille services, etc.? Have you included funds in the budget to pay for interpreters, Braille services, etc., if they are requested?

Has staff received training on the ADA and do they know how to offer accommodation, if requested? Are basic library informational materials, such as the policy manual, registration cards, and general information brochures available in alternate formats (e.g., Braille, large print, recording)?

PUBLIC PARTICIPATION IN LIBRARY DECISION MAKING

Background

To provide sufficient opportunity for the public to express opinions and provide input into library operations, policies, and procedures, both through policy and by practice, the library should encourage communication through a variety of methods (see model policy on page 54). Meetings, such as those of the library board, should be announced ahead of time and visitors should be welcome. (If the board is a governing board, state laws on open meetings may require that meetings be open to anyone.) Written and oral communications should receive prompt response from the library director or other appropriate staff member. If you truly want to know what the community is thinking, keep doors as open as possible and acknowledge calls and letters, even if you cannot make

MODEL POLICY: AMERICANS WITH DISABILITIES ACT

The (name of library) adheres to the Americans with Disabilities Act of 1990 that assures equal access to employment opportunities and access to all library facilities, activities, and programs. The library has completed a self-evaluation study and a compliance plan, both of which are available for review. Every attempt will be made to accommodate the needs of persons with disabilities and the library welcomes input from persons with disabilities about ways the library can more completely serve them. Questions about ADA compliance and complaints or suggestions about accessibility of library facilities, activities, and programs should be addressed to the library director.

Approved by (governing body) on (insert date)

_____

Signature of responsible representative

the desired changes or appease the complainant. Citizens should be part of any formal planning process and their participation in the development of library programs, services, and policy should be welcomed and encouraged.

Issues

What kinds of public meetings are held that might offer an open forum for citizen input? How can these meetings be advertised and announced? Are meetings, particularly library board meetings, subject to any open meeting regulations? Meetings of governing boards are generally required to be posted and open to citizens wishing to attend. Advisory boards may also be regulated by state law, but even if they are not subject to open meeting regulations, anyone who wishes to attend should be welcome.

Are people truly welcomed when they call for information about meetings, or when they attend them? A cliquish group will discourage participation by citizens. Too many rules about attendance (such as signing up too far in advance, submitting information ahead of time) will discourage some people from showing up.

When are meetings and public forums scheduled? Do the times

and days encourage attendance by as many affected citizens as possible? Care should be taken not to exclude any group of citizens. Opportunities for general public input should be placed at the beginning of the agenda. It is discouraging to make visitors wait until the end of the meeting to express their opinion. Some method for control of the meeting, such as *Robert's Rules of Order* or *Sturgis Standard Code of Parliamentary Procedure,* should be used.

How will the library director respond to telephone calls from citizens? Do you have an open door policy that welcomes citizens to visit without an appointment? Are telephone calls and visitors screened? Other methods to encourage input and comments might include suggestion boxes, library newsletters, a complaint hotline, or informal gatherings (brown bag lunches, coffees, etc.).

HOURS OF OPERATION

Background

Staffing levels and the budget will play an essential role in determining how many hours the library can be open each week. Hours of operation should be established to meet the needs of library users and to maximize accessibility of the collection, services, and staff. Keep in mind that schedules may need to change seasonally based on community needs (fewer evening hours in summer, Saturday hours during the school year, holiday closings). Once hours are established they should be reviewed on a regular basis but should not be changed too frequently or arbitrarily. The written policy should establish general practices, but need not indicate exact days and hours of operation. Remember that the policy sets general guidelines. If exact days and hours are included in the policy, the policy will need to be revised and re-approved every time library hours change.

Issues

Are there state, regional, or local regulations or standards regarding the minimum number of hours the library must be open? Do regulations stipulate that the library must be staffed by a specific number of employees when open? Do rules require that paid staff volunteers run the library for a stipulated period of time?

MODEL POLICY:
PUBLIC PARTICIPATION IN LIBRARY DECISION MAKING

Citizens are welcome at any open meeting of the library board either as observers or to present information and concerns to the board. Library board meetings will be held in compliance with state laws governing meetings of regulatory groups (cite appropriate law). Any member of the public who wishes to speak to the board is asked to register upon arrival, indicate group affiliation (if speaking on behalf of anyone other than self), and to limit comments and general information to five minutes. Library administration and the board welcome written documentation to support or restate information and concerns, but written documents are not required. Any group or individual wishing to place a library-related item on the official agenda for action should contact the library director one week in advance.

When public information-gathering forums are planned, care will be taken to schedule forums at times that are convenient to potential participants. If necessary, several forums may be scheduled to allow maximum input into library service decisions.

Telephone calls, letters, and visits to the library director are encouraged and the director maintains an open door policy. Appointments to meet with the director are encouraged, but not required. The library director or appropriate staff will respond to letters and telephone calls within five workdays. Comments placed in the library's suggestion box will receive a personal response, if desired. Comments of general interest may also be addressed in the library newsletter.

Approved by (governing body) on (insert date)

_____

Signature of responsible representative

Do you know what days and hours the community wants the library to be open? Have you surveyed the public to establish priority use times and potential times of high use? Does the library need to change hours seasonally or to meet specific short-term needs?

Does the library have times when staffing shortages occur? How difficult is it to fill vacant positions? Are qualified board members

MODEL POLICY: HOURS OF OPERATION

The (name of library) will be open a minimum of (establish number) hours each week. The library director, with the approval of (governing body), will determine days and daily hours of operation. A summer and holiday schedule will be established to maximize staffing during periods of heavy and light library usage.

The library will close on holidays established by (governing body) and at other times deemed necessary by the library director with the approval of (governing body). Except in case of emergencies, notice of closings will be posted in the library two weeks in advance and will be reported to the local news media.

Regularly scheduled hours of operation will be established to best meet the needs of library users and will be evaluated by survey and/or public input on a regular basis.

Approved by (governing body) on (insert date)

_____

Signature of responsible representative

or volunteers available to cover service desks when paid staff is not available due to staff vacancies, illness, vacation, or other absence?

Who has the authority to close the library in case of an emergency, such as bad weather, shortage of staff, or when problems with the building occur?

PUBLIC USE OF MICROCOMPUTERS

Background

Libraries are one of the few places where everyone can have access to microcomputers to learn their use, improve skills, try out software, or perform tasks. If the library has one or more microcomputers for public use, a written policy will help establish rules for equitable and fair access, maintain expensive and often irreplaceable equipment, and reduce the need for staff intervention (see model policy on page 58). While many libraries make stand-alone microcomputers available to the public for word processing, self-education, and use of software packages, the library is becoming the only place some patrons have available to access the Internet and other sources of electronic information. This section focuses on equitable *access* to microcomputers for personal use. If your library also offers staff-mediated access to the Internet, a separate policy may be helpful and is provided in this chapter. A more thorough look at use of the Internet by the public and acceptable use policies is included in Chapter 8, "Reference and Information Services." The complexities of networked computer systems and the rapid rate at which technology is changing and improving make it essential that all policies dealing with computers, the Internet, networked resources, and access to electronic information be reviewed regularly.

Issues

How comfortable is the library staff with the computer(s)? Has staff received adequate training and time to experiment with the computers, and to learn and maintain their skills? Will staff provide any training for patrons on basic computer skills and/or to troubleshoot software problems?

How prevalent and available are computers in your community? Do young people have significant access to computers at school? Are there businesses in the community that rent computer access time or will the library be the only available place for public use of computers?

What software is available for use on the public-access computer(s)? Will patrons be permitted to load additional programs for their own use? Will the library accept donations of software and if so, will donated software be upgraded with library funds? Does staff understand the difference between freeware, shareware, and licensed products subject to copyright?

Will patrons be required to supply their own diskettes and will fees be charged for printing? Any charges should be consistent with fees charged for similar services in the library (fax, photocopies, database searching) and should generally be based on actual costs to provide the materials or service.

How extensive do you anticipate use will be? Can patrons reserve computer time and will time be limited to allow access to patrons who are waiting? Is sufficient staff available to take reservations for computer time, orient new users, and assist with problems?

Do you want each user to sign an agreement, indicating that the person understands the rules, knows basic techniques of computer use, and will be responsible for damage caused by negligence or misuse? Can general orientation sessions be scheduled or will staff review correct operating procedures and rules on an individual basis?

INTERNET ACCESS

Background

The Internet is changing the way libraries operate. In many areas of the country, even the smallest, most remote library can have access to a multitude of electronic resources at a relatively small cost. The Internet can be used for everything from electronic communication with colleagues and friends, to more traditional library functions such as searching for cataloging information, researching reference questions, and reading newspaper articles. A written policy establishes whether the Internet will be made available to the public or be limited to staff use only. It establishes who on staff will have personal accounts, which accounts will be paid for with library funds, how much time might be devoted to monitoring listservs and newsgroups, and how access will be granted to library patrons.

If patrons will also have direct, unmediated access to the Internet, policy guidelines can be included here to determine the extent of access and establish the parameters of acceptable use of the Internet. Many libraries feel more comfortable, however, having a separate "Internet Use" policy that establishes guidelines for acceptable use. A more thorough examination of acceptable use of the Internet by patrons is included in Chapter 8.

While many of the issues in this section deal with staff use of the Internet (and therefore could have been included in Chapter 4, "Staff Conduct"), the discussion is included here because staff access and patron access are closely related. Staff access to the Internet may begin as limited use for e-mail or communication and

MODEL POLICY: PUBLIC USE OF MICROCOMPUTERS

In support of its role as an Independent Learning Center, (name of library) provides microcomputers for public use. Microcomputers and software programs permit citizens to improve computer skills, test new computer programs, and to enhance self-learning through self-improvement software (Typing Tutor, GED, etc.).

Software is purchased according to the collection development policy to support specific areas of library service. Recommendations for additional software purchases are welcome and will be handled according to the collection development policy. The library does not attempt to have the latest version of any particular software program. Programs are selected, updated, and discarded according to the collection development policy.

The library will establish and post a schedule of sessions for general orientation to the microcomputers. During the general orientation library staff will explain correct operating procedures and discuss rules for use of the microcomputer(s). All users will be required to sign a user agreement form indicating that they understand the rules established for microcomputer use and will comply with relevant copyright laws. Staff cannot provide training on computer technology or software; however online tutorials and self-instructional videos may be available for some software programs.

Users agree to observe all copyright and licensing laws and will not duplicate any computer programs or documentation unless expressly labeled as being "in the public domain" or "shareware." No personal software is to be loaded on library computer hard drives without written permission from the library director. No private files may be stored on the library computer(s) and any files left on the microcomputers will be deleted. Users will supply their own recording media (diskettes), when needed.

Computer time may be reserved for one-hour blocks of time up to one week in advance. No more than one hour per day may be reserved. When no reservation has been scheduled, the computer(s) is available on a first-come, first-served basis for one hour. Computer time and reservations are available to all patrons, regardless of age, who have a current user agreement on file. Generally, no more than two people should be sharing the computer at the same time, and each user must have signed a user agreement form.

Approved by (governing body) on (insert date)

_____

Signature of responsible representative

professional development through listservs and newsgroups, but it is rapidly becoming an essential reference tool for both staff and patrons. As staff become comfortable and competent in their own use of the Internet, they are more likely to want patrons to have at least some access on their own.

It is important to remember that the Internet is another library resource and is not inherently more valuable than other resources. Additional policies on using electronic information resources are addressed in Chapter 8.

Issues

Before access to the Internet can be made available for public use, staff must be comfortable and competent searchers. Although costs are decreasing, it may not be possible for every staff member to have an account. Which staff positions will get accounts? How much practice time will be permitted for learning about resources? Will accounts and passwords be shared? Shared accounts invite security risks and make accountability difficult to maintain but may be unavoidable in smaller libraries with very limited financial resources. (Additionally, shared accounts and passwords may be regulated and discouraged by the Internet provider.)

Will patrons be given access to the Internet through library computers? If so, include policy decisions related to patron access in this policy and in your policies on reference and information services. Will the library provide unmediated access to the Internet for patrons? Some libraries offer limited public access via menu selections on the library's online catalog. If patron access is limited, issues related to patron use can probably be dealt with in a single policy. If extensive unmediated access will be offered, library staff may feel that a separate policy on Internet use by patrons is needed.

Is Internet access primarily to be used for communications or will it also be used as a reference tool? Is staff speaking as individuals (rather than on behalf of the library) when posting to newsgroups or answering e-mail?

Will staff be assigned specific newsgroups and listservs to monitor? This avoids unnecessary duplication of effort, reduces time spent reading listservs and newsgroups, and establishes responsi-

MODEL POLICY: INTERNET ACCESS

The Internet is a tool available for providing library services. The (name of library) provides access to the Internet through individual staff accounts for professional staff, public service staff, and other staff as necessitated by job responsibilities. Staff is encouraged to use the Internet for business communications, to conduct research for patrons and library programs, and to monitor appropriate listservs and newsgroups. To ensure that a broad range of information is shared and to conserve time, staff will be assigned to monitor library-related listservs and newsgroups, and relay important information to other staff.

Staff may use Internet resources to answer reference questions and to supply information for patrons. The library will accept requests for materials, reference questions, or other communications via its general e-mail address from patrons normally served by the library. Limited public access to the Internet is provided through menu selections on the public access catalog of the library. (Alternatively, if the library offers general access to the Internet for patrons, the policy might include a statement indicating that patrons must sign an acceptable use agreement prior to accessing the Internet. A separate policy that more thoroughly addresses patron use may also be preferred.)

Personal use of Internet accounts by staff is not prohibited, but any personal communications must include the following disclaimer: "Views expressed by the writer do not necessarily reflect those of (name of library)." Personal use should not be conducted on staff time and care must be taken to avoid personal use of library resources (such as paper and diskettes). Personal files should not be maintained on the library computers. Library Internet accounts may not be used for illegal or commercial purposes.

Approved by (governing body) on (insert date)

_____

Signature of responsible representative

bility for sharing information with other staff. Is staff speaking for the library or themselves when responding to e-mail and/or requests for information on listservs?

Will the library accept e-mail from patrons? With the growing number of personal accounts, citizens can contact the library with reference questions, requests for materials, or other communications in this way. Will the library accept e-mail questions and requests for information from non-residents? The implications of providing "global" library service can be staggering. The most prudent course is usually to begin conservatively and expand services as warranted and as staff can handle increased workload and problems.

LIBRARY PROGRAMS

Background

Library programs supplement and extend the information found in library materials. Programs offer an alternative way for people to obtain and assimilate information, promote the use of library materials by focusing on topics of interest to the community, and address the role of the library as a Community Activities Center or a Community Information Center. Additionally, programming can increase traffic into the library and increase circulation of materials related to the program. Only the library and its staff may develop programs, or the library may choose to encourage programs developed by community organizations and interest groups. Policies related to programming should work toward meeting the library's established goals and roles. Policies should promote as open an environment as possible (see model policy, page 63), so consider carefully the benefits or impositions that result from requiring advanced registration, fees, or limits on audience size. Programs sponsored or co-sponsored by the library should always be open to anyone wishing to attend, as distinguished from groups making private use of the meeting room (see the policies on "Use of Meeting Rooms" in Chapter 9).

Issues

Will the library support and encourage programs developed and co-sponsored by community groups and organizations or will programs be limited to those developed and presented by library staff?

How does programming help the library meet its established roles, its mission, and goals?

Has the library endorsed ALA's "Library Initiated Programs as a Resource" interpretation of the *Library Bill of Rights*?

Can people with disabilities be accommodated in library programs in compliance with the Americans with Disabilities Act? Compliance includes access to the facilities where programs are held and interpretive services or alternative formats for handouts.

What types of programs will be approved for library sponsorship or co-sponsorship? Who will determine whether the library will co-sponsor programs developed by outside groups? Do you have a policy on "Religious Programming and Decorations"? Can outside presenters solicit business before, during, or after their program? For example, a program on financial planning may be very informative; can the person presenting the program solicit business verbally, by leaving brochures and business cards, or by having a sign-up sheet for follow-up contact?

If the program is co-sponsored by the library and an outside organization or business, who is responsible for advertising? The library has more control over how the program is advertised if staff is responsible. Extra caution must be exercised if a business or organization will be using the name of the library in its advertising.

Will registration be required, encouraged, or discouraged? Will registration be permitted for certain types of programs, such as children's storytimes, to facilitate program planning? Can attendance be limited to a specific number of attendees? How will staff handle crowds that exceed the capacity of the meeting room? Will fees be permitted for any programs?

Will attendance at programs be limited to residents of the library's service area, to patrons holding valid library cards, or will programs be open to anyone interested in attending?

Are funds budgeted for paying presenters, performers, and speakers? Can volunteers present programs for children, including preschool storytimes? Can refreshments be served?

NOTE

1. 42 United States Code Chapter 126 §12101–12213—Equal Opportunity for Individuals with Disabilities (See 62a).

MODEL POLICY: LIBRARY PROGRAMS

As part of its roles as a Preschoolers' Door to Learning and a Community Activities Center, (name of library) offers programs for citizens of all ages. Programs may be developed and presented by library staff or may be co-sponsored by the library and other community organizations. Preschool storytime programs will be presented by library staff on a regular schedule throughout the year. Other programs for children and young adults will be planned, staff time and budget permitting, during school holidays and summer vacations. Each year the library director will establish a budget for hiring performers and purchasing materials for children's programming.

Programs for adults may be scheduled throughout the year as interest warrants. Speakers from community groups and businesses may be invited to present programs on topics of general interest or of a timely nature. No funds are available to pay speakers or performers. Presenters may not directly solicit business before, during, or following a program, although cards and brochures may be left on the display table for attendees to pick up. No fees may be charged to attend any library sponsored or co-sponsored program.

Library programs are generally open to anyone wishing to attend. If space restrictions or program requirements limit the number of people who may attend, preference will be given to residents of (the library's jurisdiction). Persons attending library sponsored or co-sponsored programs are expected to adhere to the library's policies on patron conduct.

By separate action, and reaffirmed herein, the (name of jurisdiction) has endorsed the American Library Association's *Library Bill of Rights* and its interpretation, "Library Initiated Programs as a Resource."

Approved by (governing body) on (insert date)

_____

Signature of responsible representative

Chapter 6

Use of Materials

Much time and money goes into selecting, cataloging, shelving, circulating, and maintaining library materials. These items are placed in libraries to be used by patrons who may borrow the materials or use them in the library. Policies will generally be established to determine who can borrow items and under what conditions. Fees may be established for special use of some materials, and fines may be necessary to encourage the timely return of items. Patrons also have the right to use materials without public scrutiny or comment on their selections, and the right to have any record of their use of library materials kept confidential. Even the fact that the patron is a registered borrower should be confidential (and may legally be so in some jurisdictions). Policies pertaining to the use of materials should be as non-restrictive as possible to be certain that the taxpayers who support the library have as complete access and full use as is feasible.

REGISTRATION OF PATRONS

Background

Libraries are generally tax-supported institutions open to all who meet eligibility requirements. Eligibility requirements should be as broad as possible. Each person desiring to borrow materials must register, but registration policies should be kept as simple and inclusive as possible (see model policy on page 68).

The age at which children are registered for borrowing privileges is widely debated. In most states, parents must accept responsibility for items charged out to a minor. Therefore, many libraries require a parent's signature on a child's card. If parents are ultimately responsible for materials checked out by their children, libraries should encourage people to register as library users as early in life as possible. Registering young children for library cards also supports the library's role as a Preschoolers' Door to Learning.

The age of majority for legal responsibility is eighteen years old. Persons under the age of eighteen cannot be held legally responsible for library materials. Many libraries would like to issue "adult" borrower cards to young adults before the age of eighteen. Weigh carefully the fact that, while the library may not have any legal recourse in collecting fines and overdue materials, teenagers need the independence that comes from not having to ask a parent to sign for their library privileges. Additionally, consider the implications of any relevant confidentiality of records laws, intellectual freedom issues, and the *Library Bill of Rights* before requiring that teenagers have a parent's signature to obtain a library card.

Issues

What funds support the library? Library service is commonly paid for through property taxes, but taxing districts may differ from city limits. Who is entitled to borrowing privileges at no charge? Are there categories of non-residents who are also offered borrowing privileges at no charge (local government employees, students in local schools and colleges, etc.)? Will owners and employees of businesses that pay taxes be permitted to borrow materials? How will children register and at what age can teenagers register for their own cards without parental signatures?

Do state or regional laws or rules require that you extend borrowing privileges to any other jurisdictions due to reciprocal borrowing agreements, statewide library cards, or funding? Does the library wish to permit non-eligible library users to borrow materials at no charge or by paying a fee? How will the fee be established and by whom? Does paying a fee permit full library service, or will non-eligible users be limited in their use of resources and services? Some libraries only offer telephone reference or other high-use services to residents, stipulating that non-residents have paid for borrowing privileges only. If fees are to be charged, it is best to establish the conditions under which fees may be levied through the policy, but not include the fee schedule since fees may change as costs and taxes increase.

What information is required as part of the registration process? Will any voluntary information be requested for demographic purposes? How will the information be used? Exercise caution in requesting personal information unless having it serves a vital purpose and can be kept confidential.

What documentation of identification and residency will be accepted? Are there methods to accommodate persons who do not have commonly available identification? Are alternative methods of establishing identification and place of residence acceptable? It is important that documentation not be unnecessarily restrictive, especially when a specific group might be excluded from obtaining borrowing privileges (for example, accepting only a driver's license may exclude some elderly people who no longer drive; requiring a utility bill or tax statement may exclude renters). Identification may also be necessary to use special materials or services (for example "behind the desk" books, online searching services, reserve shelf, microcomputer access).

CONFIDENTIALITY OF LIBRARY PATRON RECORDS

Background

The freedom to read is one of the basic axioms of the library profession. Implicit in that axiom is the freedom to read, listen, view, and gain access to materials and information without concern that one's habits, choice of materials, or borrowing record might face public scrutiny. Law enforcement agencies, special interest groups, the media, and others occasionally seek to obtain personally identifiable information about library users. Interest by others in the library materials a patron chooses to use reflects a dangerous and fallacious assumption that what a person reads, listens to, or views equates with his or her beliefs, behavior, or potential actions. Ethically and, in many states, legally, the library must seek to protect the privacy of library users.

MODEL POLICY: REGISTRATION OF PATRONS

The (name of library) is supported primarily by taxes paid by residents of (city, county, state, or other jurisdiction). Therefore, library borrowing privileges are available at no additional charge to residents of (jurisdiction). Others may apply for borrowing privileges by paying the current fee established by (governing body). City employees, students attending schools in (city), and anyone owning real property within the (jurisdiction), may obtain a library card at no charge.

The library has a responsibility to protect the taxpayers' investment in the collection of the library; therefore identification and verification of residence is required to obtain a library card. Identification can be established through a current driver's license, school identification card, or other valid picture identification issued by a governmental agency. If no valid picture identification is available, the circulation supervisor may accept other reasonable forms of identification that establish identity. A parent or guardian must assume responsibility for materials borrowed by a person under sixteen years of age; therefore, it is the adult's identification that is required for registration of a minor. Residence is verified when the library card is mailed to the address provided. Library cards may not be forwarded to a second address and will not be distributed in person.

Demographic information may be gathered in order to plan library services. This information is used anonymously (no identifying information is compiled or reported) and is not disclosed in any way that would identify the person registering. All information provided on the registration form is protected by rules and laws (cite law) pertaining to confidentiality of records and privacy.

Approved by (governing body) on (insert date)

─────────────────────────────

Signature of responsible representative

Under limited circumstances, and following proper legal procedure, library records may be released, but this action should be based solely upon the execution of a properly prepared court order. The American Library Association has approved a number of policy statements that should be considered while formulating this policy. It may be useful for the library's governing board to adopt them or refer to them for support as part of the local policy (see model policy on page 71).

Issues

Does your state have any laws that affect the confidentiality of library records? Do you have a copy of those pertinent laws? Although many states do have laws concerning library records, some do not. Even without a state law, "all states come under the jurisdiction of federal laws—in this case, the Freedom of Information Act of 1974 and the Privacy Act of 1974."[1] Are you familiar with these statutes?

Has your governing body reviewed the American Library Association's *Policy on Confidentiality of Library Records*? Have you read the American Library Association's "Suggested Procedures for Implementing Policy on Confidentiality of Library Records"? Do you have a copy of the American Library Association *Code of Ethics*? This code states, "Librarians must protect each user's right to privacy with respect to information sought or received, and materials consulted, borrowed, or acquired." [2] Adopting the code and endorsing the ALA policies can become especially critical in supporting the rights of privacy for library patrons if your state does not have a law guaranteeing confidentiality. If local policies are not in agreement with the ALA statements, be sure that you understand the ways and reasons they differ. Even if your state has laws addressing confidentiality of records, consider endorsing these statements because they may provide an extra measure of support.

Does your state library association have statements or policies on intellectual freedom? Such documents may endorse or support the principles of the American Library Association, but usually also express areas of concern in your state. Consider adopting any state statements on intellectual freedom and privacy of patron records. State library associations may also direct you to state and local organizations, laws, and regulations that may support or affect your policies. In lieu of state laws regarding the confidentiality of patron records, check for opinions from your state attorney general or legal precedence in your state. Generally, this information will be most easily available through the state library association or your state, regional, and/or system library.

Under what exceptions or circumstances can patron records be revealed and to whom may they be released? Most laws permit disclosure of information when it is ordered by subpoena or court order. Common sense, and usually law, also permits library records to be released "because the library or library system determines that disclosure is reasonably necessary for the operation of the library or library system."[3] What penalty is stipulated for violations of confidentiality laws?

How are borrower cards for juvenile patrons handled? If cards are issued in a child's name, is the right of the child to privacy protected although a parent or legal guardian is financially responsible for the materials checked out on the card? Some states permit information about a minor child's record to be released to a parent or guardian. How will you balance confidentiality of the child's record with the parent's right to monitor and guide his or her own child's reading habits? Are juvenile library cards issued as "joint accounts," accessible by either person named on the card? Does presentation of the borrower's card imply that the presenter has the right to look at the patron records for that card?

Does your circulation system eliminate patron records when they are no longer needed for circulation control? If your circulation system is computerized, it should be programmed to delete information that links an identifiable patron with a particular item after the item is no longer charged out to the patron. If your circulation system is manual, care must be taken to completely block out or remove information that identifies the patron who used the material. Lack of adequate control or security could result in legal liability for the library and its governing authority.

Check your procedures regarding mailing overdue notices, notification of reserves, and other processes or services that might inadvertently violate a patron's right to confidentiality. Postcards that identify the items being held or the materials overdue must not be used; messages left with others or on answering machines should not disclose the title, subject of materials, or amount of fines or fees owed. Documents that record the reading habits of children during summer reading clubs or similar activities must also be kept confidential unless release is authorized by a parent or legal guardian. In some states even informing the school that a child has participated in a library program might be a breach of confidentiality laws.[4]

Know the penalties for violating your state's law regarding confidentiality (if applicable) and train staff and volunteers in the importance of maintaining confidentiality. Have legal counsel for the library review your policy for legal language and compliance with your state's laws.

MODEL POLICY:
CONFIDENTIALITY OF LIBRARY PATRON RECORDS

The (name of library) supports every patron's right to have his or her library records remain confidential. Library records include patron registration data, circulation records, overdue and reserve records, participation in library sponsored programs, record of library visits, and/or any data that contain information that links a specific patron to specific materials or services used. Each patron has individual control over his or her borrower's card and presentation of the card permits access to information about the borrower's current circulation record. Except during the actual period of transaction (circulation, maintenance of record on unpaid fines, reservation of materials), the library will not maintain a record of transactions. When no longer needed for library administration purposes, records will be expunged.

In compliance with (cite appropriate law, if applicable), no information will be released to any person, agency, or organization, except in response to a valid court order or subpoena, properly presented to the library administrator

Nothing in this policy shall prevent authorized library personnel from using library records in the administration of their regular duties. By separate action, the (name of library) has endorsed the recommendations of the American Library Association's *Policy on Confidentiality of Library Records* and the (name of state library association) "Statement on Intellectual Freedom."

Approved by (governing body) on (insert date)

Signature of responsible representative

FEES FOR SERVICES

Background

If possible, or if in keeping with the mission of the library, all library services should be funded by budgeted revenue derived from taxes or other public monies, trust funds, or donations. Some libraries adhere to a policy that states that only those services that can be supported by the budget will be offered (see model policies on page 74). If budgets are cut or costs rise unexpectedly due to price increases or higher than anticipated usage, some services may need to be reduced or eliminated.

Sometimes charging a fee is the only way the library is able to provide a service. You must balance the value and need of the service against the patron's ability to pay for them. Basic library services should always be tax-supported, but on-demand database searching, reserving materials, use of meeting rooms, and other supplemental services may only be available if costs can be recovered. Fees should be determined on a cost-recovery basis, which may include staff time, subscription costs, printing costs, consumable materials, postage, and utilities.

Consider also that services that generate revenue, even only at cost-recovery levels, may set up the expectation by funding sources that a certain amount of income will be generated by the library each year. This may make it difficult, even impossible, to stop charging for a service once you have begun to do so. Conversely, it can be difficult to begin charging for a service that was previously free if costs for that service or use of the service are higher than anticipated.

Issues

What is the library's philosophy regarding fees? Does your governing body require that fees be collected for some services? Are there state or regional laws or regulations defining basic library services for which fees cannot be charged?

Has the library adopted the American Library Association's *Bill of Rights* and endorsed its interpretation dealing with "Economic Barriers to Information Access"?

Are the funds generated by fees deposited into an account that allows the library to purchase more services or materials, or are the fees deposited into a general government fund from which the library's budget is funded? Are revolving funds, which funnel funds generated back into the program that generated them, permissible? Some fees may be more palatable to patrons if they support library services (for example, "rental" collections that allow more copies of bestsellers to be available).

Will charging a fee reduce or limit demand for a service that would otherwise be extremely popular? Would uncontrolled demand deplete limited resources? To what extent will fees interfere with the ability of children and economically disadvantaged patrons to get the information and resources they need?

Often libraries charge a fee when a new service is implemented (e.g., database searching, books on tape). These fees should be eliminated as soon as the service or materials become part of basic library services, as determined by general professional practices in your area, or when the budget permits.

How are fees established? Can you determine costs in order to set reasonable fees for the service provided? It is important to know how much a service will cost in order to determine if fees are necessary and to justify or explain how they were established.

FINES AND RECOVERY OF OVERDUE MATERIALS

Background

Uncollected fines can account for a large amount of money owed to public libraries. Of more concern to most librarians is the value of materials that are checked out but never returned. Attempts to recover materials and collect fines, in effect providing stewardship to the public's property, must be weighed against both the positive and negative publicity that might be generated by such attempts. The more non-traditional the attempts, e.g., arresting delinquent borrowers, using collection agencies, small claims court, etc. (see model policy on page 76), the more carefully the effect on public relations must be considered and the more support the library must have from both its governing authority and the community for retrieving materials and collecting fines and fees.

Sometimes someone other than the borrower may request

MODEL POLICY: FEES FOR SERVICE, 1

The (name of library) has as its mission the provision of free and open access to information in varied formats. However, there are limits to what can be provided with budgeted funds. Therefore, the (governing authority) has determined that some services will be provided on a cost-recovery basis, passing the cost of these expanded services on to the user. Fees are established when the service clearly benefits an individual user, prevents reuse of materials, or requires exceptional staff time to provide (e.g., printouts from library databases, meeting room use). Fees may also be established for supplemental services, which are not within the scope of the library's basic mission, or to enhance a service that is provided as an alternative to an existing free service (postage for notification of reserved materials, rental copies of bestsellers). Fees will be reviewed by the (governing authority) annually.

Approved by (governing body) on (insert date)

———————————————————————————
Signature of responsible representative

MODEL POLICY: FEES FOR SERVICE, 2

The (name of library) has as its mission the provision of free and unlimited access to library services and information. All services are paid for by local taxpayers, supplemented by funds from donations and trusts. It is expected that the library budget will fully fund all services and materials. No services will be offered that are not fully supported by the budget.

Approved by (governing body) on (insert date)

———————————————————————————
Signature of responsible representative

information about overdue fines and outstanding materials in order to clear up fines on their behalf (children, settling estates, insurance claims). Confidentiality laws and the right to privacy preclude disclosing more information than is necessary to clear fines. Caution must be exercised to ensure that personal reading habits are not disclosed.

Issues

Do you know how much of the collection of the library is lost each year by patrons who do not return materials and do not pay for lost items? Does the economic impact consider processing costs, including the cost to withdraw the lost item and obtain, access, and process a new one? The average real cost of processing a book can easily be anywhere from $30 to $50! What costs are associated with more aggressive attempts to retrieve materials (fees to collection agencies, additional staff, increased printing and postage) and are the costs justified when compared with the value of materials that might be returned and fees that might be collected? Have you considered carefully the public relations impact (both positive and negative) that might ensue from more aggressive collection attempts?

Are you familiar with state and local laws on confidentiality of library records and does the library have a policy on confidentiality of records? Are there circumstances that might require that someone other than the patron know what materials have fines accrued or have not been returned in order to clear records?

Does your library use an outside agency or organization to assist in the recovery of overdue materials or the collection of fines and fees? Are there state or local laws that permit the use of outside agencies (law enforcement agencies, private collection agencies) to collect fines or recover the cost of materials that have not been returned? If your library does not receive the funds from fines, weigh carefully the public relations factors if you use a collection agency to recover fine monies. Consider having the governing body (city, county, etc.) be the agency actually entering any contracts with a collection agency.

MODEL POLICY: FINES AND RECOVERY OF OVERDUE MATERIALS

Library materials are purchased for use by all citizens of (jurisdiction). The (name of library) establishes regulations for the loan of materials, including circulation periods, renewal processes, and fines for late return. The (governing body) believes that the individual who chooses to keep materials past the due date, or who refuses to settle unpaid fines or fees, compromises to some extent his or her right to privacy. The library will attempt to recover overdue materials and will notify patrons of unpaid fines and fees according to procedures established by (governing authority). Information regarding overdue and non-returned materials and past-due fines and fees may be disclosed by the (name of library) to (appropriate collection agency) when that agency has entered into an agreement with the (governing body) to recover materials or to collect fees and fines. The library will also provide sufficient information to allow any individual other than the holder of the borrower's card to settle unpaid fines or fees on that card. However, authors, titles, or subjects of lost or overdue materials will not be discussed without presentation of the borrower's card.

Approved by (governing body) on (insert date)

_____

Signature of responsible representative

RECIPROCAL BORROWING PRIVILEGES

Background

No single library can meet all of the needs of its users. Budgets, space, and the explosion of information make it impossible for any single library to own every book or item published, electronically or in print format. Sharing resources and materials extends the ability of the library to serve its customers and strengthen its collection without having to purchase every item potentially needed by a patron.

Local taxing districts have expressed more concern in recent years that reciprocal borrowing agreements reflect a balanced relationship. One library should not be expected to support inordinately a library that is not providing basic services to its primary patrons. Care should be taken to ensure that libraries in borrowing agreements offer complimentary services that expand the services of both libraries (see model policy on page 78). Some imbalances may be compensated for through regional, state, or federal programs.

Issues

What are the limits of the collection as defined by the mission statement of your library? Use the American Library Association's *Planning & Role Setting for Public Libraries* to determine the basic service roles your library will emphasize. These roles, supported by the library's collection development policy, will help you determine the limits of the collection.

What other libraries are available within a reasonable distance from yours? Do patrons regularly travel between jurisdictions for work, school, or recreation? Will the collections in other libraries provide resources not available locally?

Does the region or state have policies regarding interlibrary cooperation? Are other jurisdictions interested in cooperative agreements or reciprocal borrowing? Are local governing authorities willing to support sharing of resources? Is there a way communities that are not supporting local library services can contract with your library for services?

How will cooperative agreements increase demand for library services and materials? Can staff handle the increased traffic and any administrative or bureaucratic responsibilities?

Will citizens from other jurisdictions be able to use your library if they have lost privileges in their own library due to abuse of library services or unpaid fines? How will you confirm active, nondelinquent status?

INTERLIBRARY LOAN

Background

Because no library can meet all of the needs of every patron, nor can any library purchase every book a patron might need, a system of interlibrary borrowing and lending has evolved. Interlibrary loan permits the local library to borrow materials from other libraries in the state and around the country.

MODEL POLICY: RECIPROCAL BORROWING PRIVILEGES

Recognizing that no library collection can meet all of the informational, recreational, or educational needs of members of its community, the (name of library) enters agreements with other libraries to expand the range of materials available to our citizens. Reciprocal borrowing privileges may be extended to patrons of any library that extends privileges to residents of (your city, county, other jurisdiction). Reciprocal borrowing agreements must be approved by the (name of governing entity). Residents of (your jurisdiction) may request a current list of libraries with which reciprocal borrowing agreements exist. Due to differences in borrower registration procedures and circulation systems, borrowers may be required to register with the lending library but any non-resident fees will be waived. Privileges will not be extended, or may be limited, to persons who have lost library privileges in their own home library due to overdue materials, unpaid fines, or other unresolved problems. The (governing authority) may also enter contracts to provide library service to residents of communities that do not have library service.

Approved by (governing body) on (insert date)

_____

Signature of responsible representative

Interlibrary loan differs from reciprocal borrowing because the latter formalizes agreements between specific libraries to permit patrons to have borrowing privileges at both libraries. Interlibrary loan is a formal agreement that allows the library to borrow materials on behalf of its patron from any participating library that agrees to lend the items. Interlibrary loan is usually handled by mail and lending libraries are usually compensated for their services from state and federal funds. Interlibrary loan is not a substitute for spending local funds to develop a collection to meet the ongoing needs of local patrons and, generally, newer titles, bestsellers, and very popular items may not be borrowed through interlibrary loan. Items owned by the library, but checked out to another patron, generally should not be requested through interlibrary loan unless the item is long overdue and unlikely to be available.

If your library also participates in the interlibrary loan process as a lender, you may need to establish that in a written policy, including reference to any restrictions on lending. For example, the library may choose not to lend rare or irreplaceable materials to other libraries (see model policy on page 80).

Issues

Will interlibrary loan be restricted to residents of the library's jurisdiction or will materials be borrowed for anyone with a valid borrower's card? Will the library process interlibrary loan requests for someone who does not have a library card, but wants to use the materials in-house? Requests from children should be given the same consideration as those from adults.

On average, what is the turnaround time (include in-house processing time plus time from the interlibrary loan center) for interlibrary loan service to your library? Will requests be accepted if the patron needs the materials more quickly than the average time for receipt? Accepting a request for an item that is unlikely to be received while of use to the patron may needlessly expend staff time that could be used for other services.

Who will pay postage charges to return items borrowed through interlibrary loan? Some libraries budget for this, while others require that the patron pay return shipping costs. Is this charge permissible under state or local rules? Will overdue fines be assessed even if there is no penalty to the library? If an item is lost, will the patron be charged according to the lending library's fees? Processing costs and material replacement fees will vary greatly!

Are you familiar with copyright laws that might regulate the number of articles that can be photocopied from a periodical for a patron? Does the library have a policy regarding copyright?

Will requests be limited to a maximum number of items at one time? Electronic searching tools and access to the online catalogs of libraries around the world allow patrons to identify numerous titles that might be of interest to them. Can your staff handle numerous requests from the same patron and still serve others? Are there items that typically cannot be borrowed through interlibrary loan? It can be difficult to obtain recordings, paperbacks, reference books, microfilm, and genealogy materials through interlibrary loan.

If the library is participating in the interlibrary loan process as a lender, do you want to include the boundaries of participation in this policy? Participation as a lender may incur costs, including staff time, photocopying, mailing supplies, and postage, that may not be recovered.

MODEL POLICY: INTERLIBRARY LOAN

The (name of library) participates in the national interlibrary loan program that permits the library to borrow materials for its patrons from other libraries. This interlibrary loan service is available to all patrons whose record is clear of fines and overdue items. Books and photocopies of articles from periodicals not owned by (name of library), or that are otherwise unavailable, may be requested for loan through interlibrary loan. Recordings, microfilm, and genealogy materials may be requested but are often difficult to obtain. Items owned by the library, but checked out to another patron, may not be borrowed through interlibrary loan unless the item requested is more than two months overdue.

The (name of library) does not charge for interlibrary loan service, however the patron is responsible for charges or fines imposed by the lending library. Every attempt will be made to borrow items from libraries that do not charge fees for loaning materials. If a patron does not wish to borrow an item if charges are imposed (such as insurance fees, lending fees, photocopying charges), this must be stipulated when the request is made. Fines for overdue materials and processing costs for lost items will vary with the lending library and are the responsibility of the patron.

The library may restrict the number of items requested by an individual patron or "meter" the number of items referred through interlibrary loan when necessary to ensure fair, equitable, and timely service within the constraints of budget and staffing. This action will only be taken in consultation with the patron and alternative sources for service will be suggested. Requests that staff determines may violate copyright laws will not be accepted. Photocopies received through interlibrary loan will be stamped with a notice of copyright.

Approved by (governing body) on (insert date)

Signature of responsible representative

PROTECTION OF COPYRIGHT

Background

Copyright law is complex and includes provisions for fair use of protected materials. The library has an obligation to inform patrons about copyright laws with regard to photocopying of printed materials, duplication of audio and video materials, computer disks, and other electronic formats, and public performance of audio and video materials. In general, the borrower has the ultimate liability, if the library has made a diligent attempt to inform the patron about copyright law. Failure to make diligent effort to comply with the copyright laws could result in costly litigation.

Issues

Does the library have a copy of Circular 21, "Reproduction of Copyrighted Works by Educators and Librarians," available from the Library of Congress?

Is a statement about copyright placed on and near the photocopier(s) warning patrons that material being copied may be subject to copyright? Are other pieces of equipment in the library that are capable of reproducing materials (opaque projector, cassette duplicators) also labeled? Although no specific wording is mandated by law, the American Library Association suggests the following:

> Notice: The Copyright Law of the United States (Title 17 U.S. Code) governs the making of photocopies or other reproductions of copyrighted material. The person using this equipment is liable for any infringement.[5]

Are all copies of copyrighted materials made on behalf of a patron stamped with a notice of copyright? Again, the law does not specify wording for the copyright notice but the American Library Association has developed sample statements that libraries can copy or adapt.

Have staff and volunteers received training and information about copyright law and do they know how to determine if materials can be copied or performed publicly? Staff is generally not liable for illegal copying if the photocopier is unsupervised, that is, if staff does not make the copy for a patron.

Do you know which videos in the library collection were purchased with public performance rights? If not, check with the supplier. When in doubt, assume that there is no right for public performance.

Does the library own or have access to copyright-free art for use by patrons and staff? Does staff refrain from duplicating copyrighted materials for publicity items, decoration, use in children's programs, etc.?

Have staff been informed and encouraged to refuse to comply with requests to copy materials that are subject to copyright protection? In general, a person may make one copy of printed material for their personal use, but rarely can an entire book be copied.

MODEL POLICY: PROTECTION OF COPYRIGHT

It is the intent of the (name of library) to comply with Title 17 of the United States Code, titled "Copyrights," and other federal legislation related to the duplication, retention, and use of copyrighted materials. A notice of copyright will be prominently placed on the photocopier(s) and any other library equipment, such as cassette recorders and overhead projectors, which are capable of duplicating or reproducing copyrighted materials. Library staff will refuse to duplicate any materials if doing so would violate copyright and will, when asked, inform patrons if materials being borrowed are subject to copyright restrictions. Interlibrary loan requests will be accepted subject to copyright restrictions (see also, "Interlibrary Loan") and staff will refuse any request that would violate copyright regulations.

Audiovisual materials for which the library has purchased public performance rights will be so labeled. Items without public performance rights are for personal and home use only. Library staff will follow copyright law in selecting and using materials for public performance. Original or copyright-free art will be used to produce library publicity items or for creating displays and decorations.

Approved by (governing body) on (insert date)

———————————————————————
Signature of responsible representative

NOTES

1. Million, Angela C. and Kim Fisher. "Library Records: A Review of Confidentiality Laws and Policies." *Journal of Academic Librarianship* 11, no. 6 (January 1986): 346–349.
2. American Library Association. *ALA Code of Ethics*. Adopted June 1995 by American Library Association Council.
3. Vernon's Annotated Revised Civil Statutes of the State of Texas, Article 6252–17a.
4. Opinion provided to Herman Totten by the Texas Attorney General's staff during a telephone conversation in November 1993.
5. Simpson, Carol Mann. *Copyright for School Libraries: A Practical Guide*. Worthington, OH: Linworth, 1994.

Chapter 7

Collection Development

In conjunction with staff to assist patrons in determining their information needs, the collection is the strength of public libraries. Nowhere else in a community can the public find such a variety of information in so many formats. Materials cost money to select, acquire, maintain, use, and dispose of; therefore, items should be carefully evaluated before adding them to the collection. Policies that outline how materials purchased with public dollars are selected will focus limited funds on those that fulfill the library's mission and selected roles. Policies about gifts, donations, and deselecting and discarding of items will establish clear guidelines to avoid overwhelming the library with unusable items, while avoiding public relations problems and hurt feelings. Selection policies also provide an objective basis for evaluating items that may be the target of complaints by individuals or groups that do not think the item is appropriate for the library's collection (see model policy, page 89–90).

SELECTION OF MATERIALS

Background

The collection, including periodicals, databases and online access to information, and non-print materials, serve as the backbone of library services. Determining what to add to the collection, what to retain in the collection, and what to discard from the collection is one of the major responsibilities with which the staff is charged.

A selection policy serves as the blueprint from which the staff makes decisions. In addition to a statement delineating the library's missions, a materials selection policy should include information about the clientele to be served by the library. It should make reference to appropriate intellectual freedom documents, identify formats to be included in the collection, establish limits of the collection, and determine areas in which the library will not make purchases. The policy should also set forth who is responsible for selection decisions, what criteria will be used in making selection decisions, and how limited funds will be allocated to ensure that the needs of the entire community will be considered in purchasing decisions. It should also address how complaints or concerns about materials, both those included and those not included in the collection, will be handled (see model policy on pages 89–90).

Be cautious about promising a "balanced" collection as this may imply to the public that the library will have an *equal* amount of information on any subject or cover all viewpoints, regardless of how farfetched and inflammatory they may be. What public libraries must offer is a diverse collection that reflects major viewpoints on a variety of subjects.

Also, be cautious about using budget limitations as the rationale for not having particular items, titles, or types of materials in the collection. Those items, which might not be within the scope of the collection, might then be given as gifts. A collection development plan determines the depth and breadth of the collection and explains the types of materials that will, and will not, be added to the collection. Smaller libraries with limited budgets will probably find that their interests are best served by a brief collection development plan. Libraries with larger budgets may want detailed plans for long-term development, including guidelines by classification area. For that type of plan, refer to *Collection Development Plan for Janesville Public Library* by Carol Liddle and to *Developing Public Library Collections, Policies, and Procedures* by Kay Ann Cassell and Elizabeth Futas.

Issues

What is the mission established for your library? Have you selected basic service roles for your library from among those developed in the Public Library Association's *Planning and Role Setting for Public Libraries*? Knowing which service roles fit with the mission of your library is vital to establishing a collection development policy. A library that serves as a Popular Materials Library will develop its collection very differently than will one that has Formal Education Support Center as its major role. Materials that support the primary mission(s) of the library will receive more attention and funding than the secondary roles played by the library.

Do you know the needs of the community served by the library? What demographic information (education, income, age groups) have you collected to assist in determining community needs?

What other library or informational resources are available locally? Other nearby libraries, including school and college or university libraries, may affect your collection. What resource sharing options exist? Does the library have a policy on "Reciprocal Borrowing Privileges"? You may not need to collect as extensively in some areas if another library nearby has a strong collection and makes that information available to your patrons.

Have you surveyed the collection to determine its strengths and weaknesses? Do you have circulation statistics for representative periods in the past? Do you know what materials are used in the library but not accounted for in the circulation statistics?

Has the library board or governing officials considered endorsing the American Library Association's *Library Bill of Rights*, *Freedom to Read*, and *Freedom to View* statements? These statements strengthen support for the purchase of materials that may offend some segments of the community. Even if the governing body chooses not to endorse these documents, they may decide to reference them as supporting local decisions on selection of materials.

What selection tools are available to staff? What major selection tools will staff use to assist in purchasing decisions? If the library does not own or subscribe to sufficient standard tools, can they be borrowed from regional systems, neighboring libraries, or the state library? Is staff qualified to evaluate materials for which reviews are not available? Will certain items (local histories, patron requests, popular series) be purchased or accepted as gifts without reviews?

Will the library purchase multiple copies of high-demand items?

Will the library purchase textbooks to support school curriculums? Are there any standing orders in place that require dedicated funds every year? Are there any formats that generally will not be purchased because they are inappropriate for library use (for example, consumable workbooks), do not withstand heavy library use (for example, comic books or pop-up books), or require more staff attention than can be provided (jigsaw puzzles, art prints, or clothing patterns, for example)? You may prefer to detail the types of materials the library will purchase. Will funds be expended to purchase popular or mass-market videos and music (for which demand rises and ebbs quickly), or will limited resources restrict the collection to specialty items for which most patrons would have only occasional need (sound effects, wedding music, recorded speeches, etc.).

Will the library maintain special or unconventional collections? Art prints, sculpture, educational toys, and other items may fit within the mission of the library but usually require a great deal of staff time to handle. They usually cost more to acquire, process, and replace and may be subject to greater loss or theft than other items. Toys and puzzles quickly become well used and need to be cleaned and sanitized. Some libraries have accepted collections of cake pans, prom gowns, small tools, and fishing rods. These collections can gain a great deal of publicity for the library and may serve a real community need, especially in small towns. Remember, though, that once begun, a special collection can be difficult to maintain . Replacing, maintaining, and adding to a special collection may divert funds from the library's primary collections.

GIFTS

Background

Gifts of money, books, audiovisual materials, and other items can add significantly to the library's collection and services. A written policy establishes what items the library is willing to accept, how gifts will be handled and acknowledged, and how items can be disposed of, if not needed by the library (see model policy on page 94). Equally important, a policy will guide staff and patrons in knowing what items are not appropriate, helping the library to

MODEL POLICY: SELECTION OF MATERIALS

The (name of library) provides materials and services to support the informational and educational needs of the citizens of (jurisdiction). The primary functional roles that support this mission are: 1. Popular Materials Library and 2. Preschoolers' Door to Learning. Secondary roles are: 1. Independent Learning Center and 2. Community Information Center. These functional roles will be considered in the development of the collection, and will receive priority in the allocation of resources and funds.

Selection and purchase of library materials rests with the library director who may delegate some responsibilities to other staff members. Staff will adhere to accepted professional practices when making selection decisions. First, the recreational, educational, and informational needs of the community will be considered in selecting materials.

Before the beginning of each budget year, the director will determine how limited funds will be allocated among the major collection subdivisions (e.g., adult non-fiction, fiction, youth collection, reference, periodicals, non-print). Circulation statistics and counts of in-house use of materials will be maintained to assist in decision making. Average cost per item, as determined by the previous year's purchases and reports in library and publishing journals, will also be considered in allocating funds.

Materials will be selected based on positive reviews in professional journals or actual examination and evaluation of materials. Instead of reviews, popular demand (bestsellers, school bibliographies, local interest) may be used as the criterion for selection of materials. Items that must be updated every year may be placed on a standing order list to ensure timely delivery. Suggestions from the community for items to be considered for purchase are strongly encouraged, but materials must meet selection criteria.

The (name of library) does not attempt to acquire textbooks that support local curricula, but may acquire textbooks for general use by the public. Multiple copies of popular books (e.g., bestsellers, resume guides, tax preparation) may be purchased to meet demand. Paperback books will be purchased when available to meet short-term demand. The library will attempt to have information available in a variety of formats (book, non-book, pamphlet, magazines, etc.) when available and practical. Generally, only one copy of materials in other formats (video, compact disk, computer programs) will be purchased unless long-term high demand is anticipated. Video and audio recordings will be selected for potential long-term use to meet general interests. Regardless of an item's popularity, the library may choose not to select it, because its format is not durable enough to withstand reasonable library use, or it would require excessive staff time to maintain.

Objections to items in the collection should be made in writing to the library director. (See also the "Request for Reconsideration of Materials" policy.) Materials that no longer meet the needs of the community and no longer support the library's collection will be withdrawn and disposed of in accordance with the library's "Deselection of Materials" policy.

Approved by (governing body) on (insert date)

_____

Signature of responsible representative

avoid becoming a repository for items that cannot find a home elsewhere or that will incur substantial investments of time or money. It is perfectly reasonable to decline to accept donations if the value to the library (in time, money, and space) is not sufficient enough to balance or outweigh the cost of sorting, processing, adding records to OCLC or other databases, and storing the donated items. Remember, the cost to catalog and prepare a book to be placed on the shelf can be as high as $40. In addition, shelf space has a value, which can be calculated. Donated items should also meet the criteria established in the policy on "Selection of Materials," and may be rejected if the item would not have been acquired with library funds, had they been available (for example, due to negative reviews or unsuitable format).

The majority of items donated to the library will be used books and magazines recycled from a personal collection. Few donated books from personal collections have any monetary value, but some titles may fill gaps in the collection if they are in good condition. Occasionally the library may receive new books, special collections, and monetary donations to purchase materials. A gift policy allows the library to control its own resources (size of collection, cost of maintaining the collection, staff time) while expanding community support.

Issues

Does your library have a collection development policy? This should be in place before developing a policy on gifts since acceptance or rejection of gifts must be based on the needs of the collection.

Some libraries choose to foster an atmosphere of support by "accepting" every donation, regardless of its lack of value. This encourages community support of the library but may require a greater amount of staff time to handle materials, much of which will be immediately taken to the trash. Some libraries maintain lists of other community agencies that use and welcome outdated issues of newsmagazines, condensed or abridged versions of books, etc., and refer donors to these agencies. Do you have staff and volunteers to cull through and process large quantities of material? Has staff been trained to know what items will support the library collection and which are worth adding to the collection? How can items that are not added to the collection be handled? Does the library have used book sales or can materials be given to the Friends of the Library to sell? Free materials do cost time, money, and space!

It is not appropriate for library staff to set values for donated materials. Library staff is not skilled at establishing fair market values for tax purposes and must not do so. While a receipt should be provided that acknowledges the gift, indicating the number of items or number of bags or boxes donated, it is up to the person making the donation to set a value. Few small- and medium-sized public libraries are equipped to serve as museums or archives. In the rare event that your library chooses to accept a gift of rare or valuable books, either for display or for sale, the donor should have the items appraised by a qualified appraiser as part of the donation process. It is also best that staff not make a list of the books and other materials donated on the receipt; donors should itemize the materials if they wish to have a record.

It is preferable not to have to return unwanted items to the donor or to inform the donor as to the final disposition of the items. It is extremely cumbersome to do so and opens the library to ill will if someone must keep track of who donated every item and inform them when the item is being traded, sold, given to another agency, or otherwise discarded. Library policy should give the library sole ownership of donated items. Except in very rare instances, all items should be accepted only as outright gifts. It is generally not considered wise to accept items on "permanent loan" or to which the donor has attached conditions for use, display, care, or disposition.

Individual titles and magazines may be donated by groups, individual authors, legislators, and businesses. These gifts should be subject to your collection development policy unless the library chooses to have a special collection for works of local authors.

Donor plates are a particularly effective way to acknowledge donations but can be time-consuming. Many libraries only use donor plates for new books, memorial purchases, and other special recognitions. Before deciding that a donor plate will be inserted in *every* donated book, consider carefully the number of donated items you expect to add each year and the impact on your staff. A few minutes, multiplied a hundred times, adds up to hours that could be spent on other duties.

Decide what kinds of items and materials are acceptable and appropriate as donations. Does the library wish to accept materials in formats no longer acquired through the library budget as gifts? For example, few libraries currently purchase records, preferring audiocassettes or compact discs, but may be willing to add to their collection through donations. Will the library accept items such as 8mm film, filmstrips, or eight-track tapes if it does not have the equipment with which to use the items? Does the library wish to accept donations of toys, tools, equipment, etc.? Remember that these special collections can require a great deal of work to maintain. Does the library wish to accept gifts of art? Who will recommend which pieces of art are accepted or rejected? Is space available to house and display these items so they will be used? How do these items fit into the roles selected for library services?

Donations of used equipment, especially computers, may cost the library for repairs, maintenance, and software upgrades, which may exceed the price of purchasing new equipment.

Unless one of the library's primary roles is that of a Research Center, primary source documents or archival materials, such as private papers, manuscripts, and government records are more appropriately placed in a larger public library or an academic library. Special collections should be accepted with caution, even if the donor will provide funds to catalog, store, and secure the items, unless the library is already collecting similar items. Your policy may be able to deal with all categories of items that are not currently found in the library's collection through a general statement that is flexible.

Donations of money usually serve the library better, allowing the library to purchase items that are most needed. Does the library have a foundation, friends group, or other venue to accept financial donations? Does the library want to encourage bequests by having brochures and information available for people who might want to leave funds in their will? A brochure can also address what items the library will and will not accept through bequest and offer guidelines as to what level of bequest is required before the library will place the donor's name on the building, a room, equipment, or furniture.

MATERIALS IN LANGUAGES OTHER THAN ENGLISH

Background

In many communities, languages other than English are spoken and read by a substantial number of citizens. Library patrons or potential patrons who are more comfortable reading for pleasure and information in a language other than English can reasonably expect to find some materials for their use in the public library. Community analysis will help determine the languages other than English in which materials should be available. While it is not necessary to have a specific policy permitting the library to collect non-English language materials, some libraries find it useful to have one to validate spending tax money on items that may appear to serve a limited segment of the population (see model policy on page 96).

Issues

Does the library have a general collection development policy? Does that policy fully address serving specific segments of the community? Is this service likely to raise questions or complaints from citizens who do not understand the need for materials in languages

MODEL POLICY: GIFTS

The (name of library) welcomes gifts of new and used books, audio recordings, videos, and similar materials. Items will be added to the collection in accordance with the selection policy of the library. Once donated, items become the property of (name of library), and may be given to other libraries and non-profit agencies, sold, traded, or discarded if they are not added to the collection. Donated items will not be returned to the donor and the library will not accept any item that is not an outright gift. The library will acknowledge receipt of donated items but is unable to set fair market or appraisal values. It is recommended that the donor make a list of items donated. If items are being donated to obtain a tax benefit, it is the donor's responsibility to establish fair market value or obtain expert assistance in establishing any value. The library also reserves the right to decide when a gift added to the collection must be withdrawn.

Monetary gifts, bequests, and memorial or honorary contributions are particularly welcome. Funds donated will be used to purchase items in accordance with the selection policy of the library. Books, videos, and other materials purchased with bequests and memorial or honorary contributions will be identified with special donor plates whenever possible. If requested, notification of memorial or honorary contributions will be sent to the family of the person being recognized. Suggestions for subject areas or other areas of interest are welcome and will be followed to the extent possible.

Acceptance of donations of equipment, real estate, stock, artifacts, works of art, collections, etc., will be determined by the library board based on their suitability to the purposes and needs of the library, laws and regulations that govern the ownership of the gift, and the library's ability to cover insurance and maintenance costs associated with the donation.

Approved by (governing body) on (insert date)

_____

Signature of responsible representative

other than English? If necessary, can you clearly explain why the library needs materials in other languages? If not, consider "Ten Reasons Why We Buy Spanish Books" developed by Albert Milo, director of Fullerton (CA) Public Library.[1] His list of reasons can be applied to any language that is spoken by a significant segment of your community.

Official figures often underestimate populations of persons who prefer to speak or read languages other than English. People who speak English for daily work may still prefer to read in their first language. Do you have census and other figures for non-English- or non-native English-speaking citizens in the service area of your library? Do you know how many current and potential library users would benefit from materials in the language(s) the library will collect?

Does the library have one or more staff members who are informed, trained, and capable of meeting the needs of the non-English-speaking community? If not, who in the community could offer input in the selection of materials for the non-English collection?

Many books produced in other countries will never be reviewed in the standard library review sources. Many have weak bindings and will have to be rebound or treated as ephemeral. The library's policy may need to exempt non-English language materials from strict selection criteria and selectors may need to depend more on personal examination, patron suggestions, and non-standard selections tools. Selectors should still strive to provide the best quality materials and the highest caliber of writing available.

REQUEST FOR RECONSIDERATION OF MATERIALS

Background

Individuals or groups may question an item or items in the collection of the library. Legitimate concern about the accuracy or fairness of information must be balanced with intellectual freedom issues and the mission of the library. Complaints about material should be welcomed and handled in a dignified manner. Prompt, courteous, and proper handling of complaints can help avoid disastrous public relations problems.

MODEL POLICY:
MATERIALS IN LANGUAGES OTHER THAN ENGLISH

The (name of library) strives to have a collection that reflects the diversity of the population it serves. To that end, part of the collection development budget will be allocated to purchase materials in the preferred language of residents who are not native speakers of English. Materials considered for purchase will be evaluated as much as possible under the same guidelines and policies used for English-language materials. When necessary, staff will seek assistance in the selection of materials from appropriate community members. Citizen recommendations are always welcome and appreciated.

Approved by (governing body) on (insert date)

_____

Signature of responsible representative

At the same time, no one person or group of individuals has the right to tell others what they should read or view. A public library should have a diverse collection that includes materials that promote ideas and viewpoints that are contradictory, and perhaps even offensive, to the beliefs of members of some segments of any community. Keep in mind that while libraries should offer a diverse collection that reflects the major viewpoints on a variety of subjects, not every subject will have an equal amount of information available on all viewpoints. Challenges to materials in the library should be used to promote the library as a place where information about many ideas is available (see model policy, page 98).

Issues

Do you have a selection policy and a collection development plan? These documents explain how the library determines what is placed in the collection and how items are removed when no longer useful. Is the collection weeded regularly to remove outdated materials? It is important to have these documents and a policy on reconsideration of materials in place and supported by the library's governing authority before a complaint is filed. It is more difficult to determine procedures for handling complaints and to get support after a challenge has been made, when emotions are high.

Has the library endorsed the *Library Bill of Rights* and its interpretations and are copies displayed around the library? Do you have a copy of the *Intellectual Freedom Manual*? Are there other state or local statements on intellectual freedom? Do you know which local, state, and national organizations are available to assist you if the library is targeted by groups advocating the wholesale removal of library materials?

Are you familiar with any laws in the jurisdiction of your library that define obscenity? Are there any applicable laws that relate to the use of adult materials by minors? Do you know how the courts have defined local community standards for your area? In at least one case, the local community was defined by the courts to be the entire state, and specifically excluded the immediate city, which was more liberal than the rest of the state.

How often will the library evaluate an item for removal from the collection? Some individuals and groups have tried to overwhelm the library by repeatedly resubmitting requests for reconsideration. Does the complaint have to be submitted by a resident of the library's governing jurisdiction? Must the complainant have a library card? These issues should be considered carefully. The library serves the entire community, but the concerns of those who actually use the library may be perceived as more valid.

Are procedures in place and staff trained to handle complaints about materials? Many complaints can be resolved by respectful interest in the patron's concern and a clear, levelheaded discussion about the role of the library to provide materials for many points of view. Many libraries use a standard form that guides the patron through the reconsideration process and ensures that information pertinent to the objection is provided to library staff. This form, or a simple listing of criteria that must be included in the complaint, usually asks for contact information and information about any organization the complainant represents. Other questions might explore the nature of the objection, whether the complainant has read the entire book (or viewed the entire film), suggestions for alternative selections, and the perceived theme of the work.

MODEL POLICY:
REQUEST FOR RECONSIDERATION OF MATERIALS

The (name of library) welcomes comments and suggestions regarding the continued appropriateness of materials in the collection, especially concerning outdated materials. Suggestions will be considered and utilized by the library in the ongoing process of collection development.

Individuals may take issue with library materials that do not support their tastes and views. Staff is available to discuss concerns and identify alternate materials that may be available. If a patron's concern is not satisfied through discussion with staff, a formal, written request for reconsideration of materials may be submitted to the library director. Copies of this form are available at the reference desk or from the director's office.

The (name of library) is not a judicial body. Laws governing obscenity, subversive materials, and other questionable matters are subject to interpretation by the courts. Therefore, no challenged material will be removed solely for the complaint of obscenity or any other category covered by law until after a local court of competent jurisdiction has ruled against the material. No materials will be knowingly added to the library collection that have been previously determined to be in non-compliance with local laws.

For a request for reconsideration to be considered, the form must be completed in full. The patron submitting the request must be a resident of the (library's jurisdiction) and hold a valid borrower's card. The director will respond, in writing within thirty days of receipt, to the patron's request for reconsideration. The response will indicate the action to be taken and reasons for or against the request. An item will only be evaluated for reconsideration once in a twelve-month period.

Approved by (governing body) on (insert date)

_____

Signature of responsible representative

DESELECTION OF MATERIALS

Background

The cycle of service requires that while materials are added to the collection, some must also be discarded. A good collection is hampered by outdated, inappropriate, shabby items that may camouflage useable items while making library shelves look full. A policy about weeding library materials should detail criteria for deselecting, pinpoint decision-making responsibility, and establish proper methods for disposing of discarded items. Deselection should *not* be used as a way to avoid dealing with a patron complaint about materials or to respond to censorship challenges (see also "Request for Reconsideration of Materials" policy).

Issues

Do you have a written collection development policy? This is the first step in understanding the direction that the library collection should be taking. Weeding can provide feedback on the collection's strengths and weaknesses and the information collected during the weeding process should be considered in revising a yearly plan for allocating collection development funds.

Have you identified the major public service roles of the library? Significant changes in the service roles of the library may affect decisions about keeping or discarding certain items.

Who will be responsible for weeding the collection? Although final responsibility for the collection rests with the library director, a good rule of thumb is to have the same people who are responsible for selecting the material also be responsible for its removal.

Mistakes and indecision are inevitable in any process based on judgment. Standard evaluation tools and specialized bibliographic aids can also help determine potential future usefulness and identify classic titles in a particular field of study. *The CREW Method: Expanded Guidelines for Collection Evaluation and Weeding for Small and Medium-Sized Public Libraries*[2] offers formulas based on the age of the book (last copyright), maximum permissible time without usage (circulation), and various negative factors (inaccuracy, beyond repair, trivial, etc.). Many libraries use the CREW guidelines to assist in making weeding decisions. Do you know who in the community can be called on to help with areas of the collection that are tougher to evaluate? Final decisions always rest with the library director but experts can often help staff understand specialized fields.

Does the library's governing authority have laws, ordinances, or policies governing how property can be disposed? Sometimes all items removed from the library collection must be sold at public auction. Since this is a very unsatisfactory way to dispose of library materials, try to get authority to give the items to a Friends of the Library group, offer materials to other libraries, literacy groups, or social service agencies, or sell discarded items directly in the library. Avoid giving items to individuals, even if local regulations do not prohibit this, because doing so can lead to charges of favoritism or the appearance of misuse of funds.

MODEL POLICY: DESELECTION OF MATERIALS

Materials that no longer fit the stated service roles of the library will be withdrawn from the collection. This may include materials that are damaged, include obsolete information, or are no longer used. Decisions will be based on accepted professional practice, such as those described in *The CREW Method*, and the professional judgment of the library director or designated staff. When necessary, local specialists will be consulted to determine the continued relevance and reliability of materials.

Items withdrawn from the collection will be disposed of in accordance with local law, which permits discarding into the trash, recycling of paper, or transfer to the Friends of (name of library) for sale. No items may be sold or given directly to individuals or groups. Discarded magazines and newspapers may be given to other area libraries or social service agencies at the discretion of the library director.

Approved by (governing body) on (insert date)

_____

Signature of responsible representative

NOTES

1. Milo, Albert. "Ten Reasons Why We Buy Spanish Books," *Public Libraries* 5, no. 10 (November-December 1995): 340–341.

2. *The CREW Method* by Belinda Boon updates *The CREW Manual* by Joseph Segal, published by the Texas State Library in 1976, and reprinted in 1980 as *Evaluating and Weeding Collections in Small and Medium-Sized Public Libraries* by the American Library Association.

Chapter 8

Reference and Information Services

The services that the library provides, including reference services, reader's advisory, access to information, and programs, can play a role even more vital to the community than the library's collection. Without the services provided by trained and educated staff, the library would be nothing but a building full of materials. No library can be all things to all people.

The roles the public library selects will influence the level and types of reference and information services provided. A public library that has elected to be a Reference Library will offer a more extensive reference collection and a wider array of reference services than will a library that is primarily a Popular Materials Library. Computer networks and the Internet are also greatly expanding the services libraries can provide. Patrons can often search the library catalog after hours, order full-text copies of articles through electronic databases, and download information from the Internet. Policies about services support the roles of the library and enable the community to know what the library staff can do to help them with their educational, informational, and recreational needs.

REFERENCE AND INFORMATION SERVICES

Background

Reference and information services can be an integral part of public service, especially for those libraries that have identified their roles as Community Information Center, Formal Education Support Center, Independent Learning Center, or Reference Library. Regardless of the primary roles selected, every public library provides some level of reference service.

Reference service can be provided by telephone, mail, e-mail, fax, or, more commonly, in person. Staff should endeavor to serve each person uniformly and fairly, usually providing service first to the person who has taken the time to come into the library. All questions should be considered legitimate, and no preference should be given, nor should service be withheld based on age, type of question, status of the requester, etc.

Staff time and workload may require that some levels of service be established. For example, staff workload might limit the amount of time staff can spend researching quiz or contest questions, although caution must be taken to avoid probing too deeply into the reasons a patron has for wanting the information. Genealogical research can also take a great deal of time, and some libraries limit the amount of time staff can spend searching old city directories, local newspapers, and other sources. Some libraries may want a separate policy dealing with homework assistance (see policy in this chapter). Consider carefully what services will be restricted and keep in mind that reference service may be the most visible service that the library provides. Above all, develop policies that support the library's selected roles, maximize available resources, and assure equitable access to assistance. Policies should not be based on age or other discriminatory factors.

Reference staff needs to exercise caution when providing legal, medical, or consumer information. Information should be supplied, but advice or interpretation of the information must be avoided. When appropriate, staff should make referrals to other community groups or organizations that may be able to serve the patron more completely.

Issues

Has the library selected Reference Library as one of its primary or secondary roles? What is the workload at the reference desk? How many staff members work on the reference desk? Are all questions, including directional and general information, handled through one service desk? Does the library have active telephone reference service or is most of the work done in person? Are reference questions received electronically or by mail? Priority is usually given to those patrons who come into the library before those who call, but staff will still need to be assigned to handle questions received through other channels. Do you want to establish guidelines that limit how much time will be spent helping a patron over the telephone?

Have staff members been trained to do reference and research work? Is training available for those staff members who do not have a degree in library science or who have not taken formal reference classes? Are procedures in place so that less skilled staff or volunteers know when to refer the question on to another staff member?

What level of research is performed at the reference desk? Has the library selected the role of Research Center as one of its primary or secondary roles? Does the library have a system for referring questions that cannot be answered locally to another library or to a regional or state reference back-up service? Good customer service requires that the staff member verify that the patron is satisfied with the information located and make referrals or offer suggestions for further research, if necessary.

Will reference questions be accepted by electronic means, such as e-mail and fax? Some simple questions of a factual nature (e.g., population of a city, definition of a word) may be understandable without a reference interview, but often questions that appear to be simple become more complex. If questions are accepted electronically, will they be answered in the same manner? It can take more staff time when responses must be typed into a computer, but e-mail can be an effective way to respond to patrons quickly and efficiently. Will questions be accepted via e-mail from non-residents? Library Web pages that invite local residents to send reference questions via e-mail may also appear to invite questions from around the world. Providing worldwide reference assistance may not be feasible. Will materials be copied and faxed to patrons? Does the library have a policy on faxing materials?

Can reference staff make long-distance calls to obtain information needed to answer a reference question? Is a community

MODEL POLICY: REFERENCE AND INFORMATION SERVICES

The reference staff at (name of library) endeavors to provide accurate information and materials in response to requests from library users in an efficient, courteous, and timely manner. In order to ensure that quality service is provided, only staff trained in providing reference service will work at the reference desk. Questions are generally answered in the order received, with priority given to questions asked by patrons in the library.

Services available through the reference desk include information services (answers to specific questions, call number and ownership of a specific book, recommendations on subject materials); instruction on the use of the library and library materials (indexes, online services, catalog, reference tools); bibliographic verification of items requested (title, author, publisher, ISBN, price); reader's advisory (suggestions on books to read, videos to view, recordings to hear); referral to community services; and assistance in locating materials.

Before responding to a reference request, staff must understand the question completely. When answering specific information questions, staff will always cite the source of the answer. Personal beliefs, opinions, and experience are generally not acceptable sources of answers to reference questions but, if given, will be appropriately identified. Staff will accompany the patron to the location of the desired material in the library and confirm that the information meets the patron's need.

Telephone reference service is usually limited to supplying readily available information that does not require extensive research and that can be accurately imparted over the telephone. Extensive research that requires selection of appropriate materials, interpretation of data and sources, or analysis of information is best performed by the patron. Detailed information, especially that which is subject to analysis or interpretation, will not be relayed over the telephone. Samples of available materials can be gathered and held for patron pick-up.

Staff cannot photocopy materials to be mailed except under circumstances authorized by the library director (for disabled patrons who cannot come to the library, for other libraries, etc.). Telephone reference questions that can be answered quickly (two or three minutes) without affecting service to patrons in the library should be handled while the patron waits. Questions that require more time to answer, or that are received while other patrons are waiting in the library, will be handled as callbacks. All callbacks will be cleared by the end of the day or the patron will be notified of the delay. Privacy and concern for accuracy of information will be considered when leaving messages on answering machines or with another household member.

Additional care and caution must be exercised when providing legal, medical, or consumer information. To avoid misunderstandings, it is preferred that patrons visit the library to review this type of information, rather than receiving the information over the telephone. Reference staff will provide definitions, quote material verbatim, and direct patrons to information sources. Staff will not offer advice or opinions, condense or abstract information, or suggest a course of action or diagnosis. Staff will provide the source and copyright date for legal and medical information.

All requests for reference information are confidential. Reference staff may consult with each other when necessary to serve the patron or consult with staff at other libraries, agencies, and organizations. Questions are tallied for statistical purposes and may be compiled to assist in staff training. In all cases, patron confidentiality and privacy will be maintained.

Approved by (governing body) on (insert date)

_____

Signature of responsible representative

information file maintained for referrals, especially when questions involve legal, medical, or psychological information?

If searching online databases incurs costs to the library beyond flat-rate licensing fees, the library may want to have a separate policy on database searching to ensure that all patrons have equitable access to limited resources. Similarly, many libraries that offer unmediated patron access to the Internet want to have a separate policy that establishes appropriate use of the Internet connection.

Will reference and information transactions be recorded for statistical use, collection development, training, or other purposes? Be careful not to compromise patron confidentiality and privacy while assisting patrons in the library, when seeking assistance from other staff, specialists, and organizations, and when staff must call a patron back with answers and information.

HOMEWORK ASSISTANCE

Background

It is important to recognize that homework assistance can be requested by anyone of any age; homework assignments are not limited to children and youths. The policy regarding homework assistance should be the same for any student, including adult learners.

Each library must examine its own missions and determine the extent of assistance reference staff will provide with homework. Depending on philosophy and the roles selected for library service, the library can answer the questions asked, help patrons find the answers, or teach patrons how to use library resources to find the answers on their own.

Issues

Discussion should include ways in which homework assistance differs from other reference questions. Has the library selected as one of its roles that of a Formal Education Support Center? Should reference assistance be offered to help the patron find the answer or to teach the patron how to use library resources? Will the level of service or the extent of assistance with homework be different for in-library patrons, versus telephone questions?

How will staff determine if the question is related to a homework assignment? Contact and cooperation with area schools is helpful, but often hard to establish. It may be difficult to discern homework questions from other reference requests until the same question is heard several times.

Have you discussed homework assignments and assistance with the schools in your service area? Does the school district offer after school homework help? Are there other groups or organizations in the community offering intensive homework help? Could another community group offer this service in the library? This would free staff while still making the service available.

MODEL POLICY: HOMEWORK ASSISTANCE

Homework questions from students, regardless of age or grade level, will be answered in the same manner as any other reference question (see also the policy on "Reference and Information Services"). Priority will be given to questions asked by patrons in the library. Telephone assistance will be limited to short, factual questions that can be answered without interpretation of materials. Materials may be pulled from the shelves and held for patron pick-up. If a teacher informs the reference desk staff that the search process, and use of research materials located, are part of the assignment, staff will defer to the teacher's request and limit assistance to helping students with their research without supplying answers.

Elementary grade students needing intensive assistance with their homework (e.g., interpretation of assignment, tutoring, explanation of math problems, etc.) will be referred to the school district's homework assistance program.

Approved by (governing body) on (insert date)

———————————————————————————

Signature of responsible representative

FAXING

Background

Fax machines have been around for some time and are available even in the smallest communities. Libraries may look at faxing information as a way of sharing resources with other libraries. It may also provide a way to extend reference services, especially to those who cannot come into the library or who need information more quickly than it can be delivered by other means. Faxing costs the library staff time, and requires photocopying. Telephone charges may also be an issue. Acting as a fax service, where patrons request that the library fax or receive items that are not library related, can be more time-consuming and place a burden on staff that may be beyond the scope of the library's mission.

Issues

Can staff handle the anticipated workload associated with fax service? Does your budget include funds to cover costs of this added service? At what level?

Is your fax telephone number published and available to patrons who might want to fax questions or correspondence to the library? Publishing a fax number in directories may result in the receipt of many junk faxes, which cost paper and toner and tie up the fax machine. Should the library fax number be included on library promotional materials distributed to patrons?

Will your staff accept faxed reference questions from patrons or from other libraries? Simple, factual questions may be handled via fax, but longer, more involved questions usually require that a reference interview be conducted.

Does your service area include places from which the library is a long-distance telephone call? If it does, patrons may prefer to fax requests, rather than incur extensive long-distance charges from lengthy telephone calls. Can the library budget support long-distance calls to fax information to patrons?

Are other businesses available in your community that will send and receive non-library-related faxes for patrons? Many libraries choose not to compete unnecessarily with local businesses, but in very small communities the library may own the only publicly available fax machine.

Do you have a policy on copyright and are staff familiar with copyright law? Faxing usually involves making a photocopy first. Copyright principles require that this photocopy be destroyed once the fax has been sent; it may not be kept for future use.[1]

Will the library try to collect fees for photocopies that were made in order to fax information to the patron? This could create more work than warranted if the library must prepare and fax an invoice with the document. However, if fax requests will take more of the library's budget than can be afforded, a method for collecting fees might be needed.

MODEL POLICY: FAXING

Fax service is provided by the (name of library) when the information requested is brief and readily available in printed form. Staff cannot conduct extensive research, compile information, or gather data from a variety of sources to be faxed. Fax service will be limited to brief, readily available information provided as part of the reference services of the library. Materials and information may be requested by incoming fax, and requests will be treated in the same manner as telephone reference questions.

Staff will adhere to copyright restrictions when faxing materials, and a copyright violation warning will be affixed to the front page of copyrighted materials being faxed. Staff may refuse to fax materials that would violate copyright laws.

Fax telephone calls will be made only within the local dialing area except for those made to other libraries. Requests for fax services that are not related to library business will be referred to local fax businesses listed in the telephone directory. Incoming faxes will not be accepted on behalf of patrons, except for those originating from another library. Because collecting for photocopying material to be faxed would be difficult, no charges will be made for photocopies associated with fax service. Photocopies made to facilitate faxing will be destroyed after use.

Approved by (governing body) on (insert date)

_____
Signature of responsible representative

PHOTOCOPYING

Background

Today, photocopiers are standard equipment in most public libraries. They offer patrons a convenient way to copy information from reference books, magazines, and other non-circulating materials. The library photocopier will generally be older and less sophisticated than those found in a copy center or print shop, and should not be expected to substitute for professional copying services. Photocopiers also may reduce mutilation of library materials, because

cause they offer patrons a way to get a copy without cutting up periodicals and reference materials.

Issues

How will the fee for photocopies be established? Fees should be low enough (cost recovery) to encourage patrons to copy materials rather than mutilate books and periodicals. Some libraries offer a small amount of free copying to discourage theft and mutilation of materials. Children, who rarely have money for photocopies and may not have considered the need to copy information, are often also offered a few free copies for school needs.

Are you familiar with copyright restrictions and do you have them posted by the photocopier? Does the library have a policy on copyright?

How will staff handle requests for copies when the equipment is not working? If a business with a photocopier is nearby, patrons might be permitted to take items there to be copied. Will refunds be given for poor copies? Is the copier to be self-service (except for patrons with disabilities that prevent their making their own copies) or will staff make copies, collate, and double-side print? Keep in mind that liability for copyright violations may increase if staff performs or closely supervises copying.

DATABASE SEARCHING

Background

Most libraries now have some access to information in electronic formats. This may include CD-ROM products that supplement or replace print indexes, CD-ROM products that include full-text copies of magazine articles, online searching tools, and full or limited access to the Internet. CD-ROM products usually are leased or purchased for a flat rate, although some full-text products may charge a fee for each article actually printed. Online searching frequently has a per-search charge, a per-hit fee, or a fee to download data. These fees may be absorbed as part of the library's budgeted services, or may be charged to the patron. Cooperative networks may provide access, at no cost to the local library, to databases as part of regional or statewide licenses. Some licenses of-

MODEL POLICY: PHOTOCOPYING

The (name of library) provides a photocopier for public use, primarily to facilitate using non-circulating materials such as reference books, magazines, newspapers, and local history materials. Fees for the copier are established by the board and reviewed annually. As a deterrent against mutilation and theft of library materials, a patron may make up to five free copies per day from non-circulating materials.

Photocopiers are self-service and, with the exception of assisting disabled patrons, staff is not available to make copies. Staff will not knowingly violate copyright law when assisting with the copier. Patrons using the photocopier must adhere to the U.S. Copyright Law when copying materials subject to copyright.

The library attempts to maintain its equipment in good working order, however the library is not a print or copy shop. Copies are for convenience only and those seeking print quality copies (such as for resumes, business correspondence, etc.) will be directed to local printing businesses. The library will reimburse only for the first copier malfunction or poor quality copy. At the discretion of the staff, patrons may be permitted to take materials to a nearby copy center if the copier is out-of-order. Decisions will be made based on the immediacy of need, the type of material, and anticipated length of time that the copier will be out of service.

Approved by (governing body) on (insert date)

_____

Signature of responsible representative

fer unlimited access to some databases, but charge the consortia or sponsoring agency per search for others. Even products that do not have an associated cost for the search will have costs to the library for paper and toner to print out search results. Policies regarding the use of electronic resources and databases should allow as much flexibility as possible, while maintaining control of costs and avoiding unreasonably massive printing. All patrons, including children, should have equal access to online and electronic services under the same conditions.

Issues

Has the library endorsed the American Library Association's interpretation of the *Library Bill of Rights* on "Access to Electronic Information, Services, and Networks"?

Does the library own, lease, or have access to databases or electronic information resources? What are the costs associated with these resources? Are the resources purchased or leased at a flat rate or are charges made per use? Can the per-use charges be easily determined? Do you want to establish some fee-based services, while allowing library staff to use database searching as a tool at no charge to the patron when doing so best meets the research needs?

Is staff available to conduct online searches on behalf of patrons or are the searches self-service? Mediated searches take up staff time but may result in more efficient, and therefore less expensive, searching. Is similar information available through other library resources? In other words, does the electronic resource make searching quicker and more current, or is it the only source of similar information available in the library? Some libraries absorb search costs if it is the only source of information, but may pass along costs for searches conducted at the patron's request for expediency.

If the library offers access to the Internet, do you have an Internet policy outlining what services will be provided, who is entitled to access, and at what level of access? If patrons will have unmediated access to the Internet, do you want to have a separate policy on acceptable use of the Internet?

How many search stations are available? Do you want to set a time limit on searching because patrons queue up to use the searching tool(s)? Often when service is first offered, patrons are attracted to the novelty and search time is monopolized. Can patrons schedule time to conduct their database searches? Are staff or volunteers available and trained to provide instruction on how to formulate search strategies, use electronic resources, and navigate the Internet?

Can patrons print out search results? Do you want to or need to charge for paper for printouts? Can patrons download search results to their own diskettes?

MODEL POLICY: DATABASE SEARCHING

In accordance with the (name of library's) policy on collection development, information may be acquired in electronic format. Whenever possible, and if economically feasible, the library will acquire electronic information that allows use to be unmetered. If this is not possible, charges will be established by (governing authority) on a cost-recovery basis for electronic searching and retrieval of information and documents, when the library is charged for such services on a per-search or per-hit basis. Charges will also be established for printing search results. Patrons may supply their own blank, formatted diskette for downloading of information, if permitted by the electronic resource. Search results may also be forwarded electronically to a patron's e-mail address if this function is supported by the electronic resource.

Search time on unmediated electronic resources may be limited to fifteen minutes per patron when others are waiting to use the equipment. Electronic resources are generally only one available source of information and reference staff will help patrons locate other library resources that will meet their information needs. Staff is also available by appointment to discuss search strategies, provide instruction on how to use the electronic resources, and offer suggestions for other resources that may be useful.

Approved by (governing body) on (insert date)

_____

Signature of responsible representative

INTERNET USE POLICY

Background

While it has dramatically changed the way people can access information, the Internet is both another research tool and another service that the library may or may not offer to the public. With a computer and an Internet account, it is possible to search millions of computers and retrieve thousands of pieces of information. Some of the information retrieved is accurate and valid, some is erroneous, inflammatory, or offensive, and, yes, some of it may be pornographic, racist, disgusting, or dangerous. However, "one percent or less of all materials on the Internet is obscene and much of it requires a credit card to access."[2]

Staff, patrons, parents, the community, and governing authorities will be more comfortable if policies are in place to establish appropriate and acceptable use of the Internet in the library (see model policy on pages 122–123). Policies may or may not result in limitations on service, but the results of conscious and deliberate decisions, arrived at after research, input, thought, and consideration will benefit all who are involved in providing or using library resources. Regardless of the decisions made, you are strongly urged to have your policy in place before the first patron logs into the Internet in your library! Because of the currency of the issues, the emotions connected with the topic, and the rapidly changing environment, this section is longer than most of the others provided in this book. Keep in mind that technology continues to change; Internet policies may need to be reviewed more frequently than others.

Most libraries offer access to the Internet for staff before opening up the service to the public. Staff must be comfortable with the technology before they can assist patrons. Training and practice time is critical to attaining proficiency and ongoing opportunities are essential to keep skills up-to-date. (See also the policy on "Internet Use.")

The first point to consider is whether the library will provide Internet services to the public. Because the Internet is available to anyone with a computer, some people have questioned whether the library has any role in providing access. Indeed, a few have even postulated that by its very nature the Internet will make public libraries obsolete. The reality is that for those who cannot afford personal access or who require only infrequent access, the library may provide the only point of access. As more government agencies and other organizations discontinue publication of information in paper formats, those without Internet access will be extremely disadvantaged. Even when paper copies are made available, electronically delivered information is almost always more timely and more current (but not necessarily the "official" version for legal use). An excellent discussion for trustees and library board members about Internet connections is "Do You Dare?"[3] Very succinctly, this document offers guidance for board members and raises questions to consider.

Librarians are information specialists, trained to formulate search strategies that ensure retrieval of a manageable amount of relevant information. Quantity means nothing if the information is not valid. Librarians help patrons evaluate the source of information, its accuracy and reliability, and suggest alternate resources. We do this with print resources and we do it with electronic resources, including the Internet. Internet services change at lightning speed; as difficult as it may be for library staff to keep up with changes, it is even more difficult for the average patron who uses information resources only occasionally.

Decisions about patron access to the Internet and the extent of Internet services the library will offer will depend on a number of factors. The roles your library has selected always influence the services provided. Libraries with the role of Community Information Centers will probably choose to mount Web pages offering information about community events with links to organizations and groups in the community. A library that is primarily a Preschoolers' Door to Learning may offer a limited menu of Internet services. Available public service staff, their computer abilities and level of comfort with technology, and the volume of workload will also help shape decisions about Internet access and assistance.

There are no right or wrong answers, and few questions are unanswerable. It is unlikely that your library will face any situation that others have not also had to deal with. Examine the other policies your library has established. Decisions that have already been made about charging for services, age restrictions, and assisting patrons will influence many aspects of your Internet policies. Decisions about limits on printing or charges for paper probably have already been established in other library policies (see policies on "Database Searching" and "Public Use of Microcomputers"). Before making local decisions, use the Internet to get information about what other libraries are doing. Lake Oswego (OR) Public Library maintains a Web site (*http://www.ci.oswego.or.us/library/*

poli.htm) that analyzes Internet policy elements, providing summary and detailed information about policy elements along with links to public library Internet policies by state, size of population served, and year the policy was developed.[4] Other sites archive acceptable use policies, provide updated information on legislation affecting Internet access, evaluate filtering and security software systems, and offer links to training resources and other useful information.[5]

Issues

Do you and your staff, the library board, and governing authorities understand the Internet and how it works? Are you familiar with the range and multitude of information available? Are you comfortable with the relatively ungoverned nature of the Internet? It is not a company or agency controlled by any individual person. Before establishing policies on patron use of the Internet, staff and the library's governing body should clearly understand the Internet's potential and the inability of any organization to fully monitor or control access to the information provided through this network of computers. Early in the process, provide demonstrations of the Internet for library staff and decision makers (later, of course, you may also want to offer demonstrations for the public). Many misconceptions exist about the seemingly infinite capabilities of the Internet. Be certain that all who are involved in the development of policy understand terminology, concepts, and capabilities (chat room, e-mail, MUDs and MOOs). Does everyone understand the differences between graphic capabilities and text-only access to the World Wide Web? If you cannot explain these terms and concepts, find someone who can.

What Internet functions will be available to patrons? Will the library act as an Internet provider, allowing patrons to establish accounts through the library? Do you have staff and resources to accommodate this level of service? Are other Internet service providers available in the community?

How will you deal with issues on pornography, sexually explicit sites, and other objectionable materials that are available over the Internet? Are you familiar with federal, state, county, and local ordinances that might affect your policies? The Supreme Court ruled on June 26, 1997, that the Communications Decency Act (CDA) is unconstitutional because it violated the First Amendment protections of free speech. Even so, obscene speech and child pornography is not protected by the First Amendment,[6] but material that might be indecent is not de facto also obscene. State laws or local ordinances may restrict materials that might otherwise be protected.[7] Patrons or staff who display pornography to others, distribute child pornography, etc., may be committing criminal acts or acts of sexual harassment and should be dealt with through the legal system. Some libraries include a statement advising patrons about laws dealing with obscenity and child pornography; before they can access the Internet the patron must take action indicating that he or she has at least seen the warning. The American Library Association offers question and answer information about CDA at its Web site (*www.ala.org*) with links to other associations and organizations that have an interest in the Internet. It is important that library staff and board members keep up with changes in cyberspace law and consult with legal counsel before making decisions.

Have the staff and the library's governing authority read and discussed "Access to Electronic Information, Services, and Networks: An Interpretation of the Library Bill of Rights"? Are you and the library's board or other governing authority familiar with various filtering software packages? Carefully consider any decision to use filters. On July 2, 1997 the American Library Association adopted a resolution that states that the use of filtering software by libraries violates the *Library Bill of Rights*. A copy of that resolution is provided in Appendix C of this book.

Libraries are as likely to be sued for filtering as they are of facing legal difficulties for not filtering. "The Internet has been held to be a 'public forum' which means that expression communicated through it enjoys the highest level of protection from government interference."[8] The use of filtering software by the library probably would impede free speech. Even if you have decided not to filter, an understanding of how each software package works and comparison of capabilities and limitations will aid in explaining your decision. Filtering devices can provide a false sense of security for concerned parents and, in the opinion of some, could open the library to liability when the "protection" fails.

While the Internet has the capability to support a variety of uses, the library should select those uses that fit the roles established for service and the community's needs. Some uses and some users may be accorded priority, while the library may elect to restrict or eliminate other uses. Can patrons initiate e-mail from the library's computers to send to other accounts? Will access to chat rooms and MUDs (or other multi-user simulation environments, virtual reality sites, or interactive games) be permitted? Do these functions further the mission of the library or fulfill one of the service roles of the library? Can patrons download files to disks or e-mail files to their own accounts? Permitting patrons to download files may reduce the demand for printing. Again, if you do not understand these functions and their capabilities, find someone who can explain and demonstrate them for you. (Often your state, regional, or system library has staff who can assist you; if not, contact local colleges and high schools or community business partners.) Use for research and homework purposes may take precedence over playing games on the Internet. Visits to chat rooms may not be permitted at all. Library cardholders may be able to reserve searching time or make appointments to use the terminals for research.

Does the library have the staff to monitor Internet use closely? An elaborate system to "qualify" users, reserve time, assign specific computers to patrons, and clear or reset terminal preferences will not be easy to handle if staffing levels are low. Without sufficient staff, you may need to limit the variety of uses and invest in more security devices to protect the integrity of the computer or its network. Day-to-day maintenance and regular checks on the system will take staff time; add to that the time needed to reset computers, scan for computer viruses, work with patrons, handle time slots or mediate disputes about waiting times, disperse headphones, diskettes, papers, or other supplies, and unlock and lock disk drives. Is staff time available to handle each function? If not, look for alternatives that permit the most access for patrons within the limitations of the budget of the library. Volunteers can certainly help, but remember that once a service level is set, it can be difficult to pull back. Start conservatively and expand services as resources permit.

Will staff conduct formal or informal Internet training for patrons? Can printed and electronic resources be purchased or developed to address basic skills and answer routine questions about searching? Are staff or volunteers available to offer training classes or to "train on the fly" as users need help?

Will library staff establish specific starting points for searches on a home page or front-end menu? These can help by pointing to frequently used sites and can reduce searching time and misuse by leading inexperienced or casual users to sites that fit with the library's mission and roles, including kid's pages and other age-appropriate sites. Many libraries also place disclaimers that patrons must read on the opening screen before proceeding into the Internet. Disclaimers remind patrons that policies have been established, reinforce the library's purposes in providing the level of access available, and may provide some degree of protection from liability if a patron encounters offensive material or retrieves erroneous information. Disclaimers may also alert patrons to the need to protect their home computers from viruses if files are downloaded from the Internet. Always have disclaimers checked by legal counsel.

Have you determined where Internet computers will be located? For example, can computers be placed in several locations around the building or will they be consolidated into one area such as a computer room? Decisions about location may impact decisions about monitoring use, training and staff assistance, or the need for volunteers, as well as decisions about filtering sites, restricting use by minors, or rationing supplies. Location may also affect the privacy of patrons who are using the computers.

Will children be permitted to use the Internet on an equal basis with adults? The *Library Bill of Rights* and its interpretation on "Free Access to Libraries for Minors" endorses the right of youth to have unrestricted access to information and library resources. Has the library's governing authority endorsed or adopted these statements? Will parental permission be required for children to use the Internet? Before establishing a separate process for Internet use, consider revising the application for a library card to include a statement of parental responsibility for all library materials and services selected or used by their child.[9] What impact would restricting access to minors have on the ability of children to get information they need or want? What impact will monitoring approved use by children have on staff time and the staff's ability to help other patrons? Do you have information available for parents on child safety on the Internet? The National Center for Missing and Exploited Children has an excellent brochure that can be purchased or downloaded from the Internet. Many libraries link to this document from their home page to help parents understand how the Internet works, the value of resources available, and ways to help their child stay safe.[10] Remember that the library staff can not act *in loco parentis*; parents can restrict the materials and services accessible to their child, but only for their child.

MODEL POLICY: INTERNET USE

As part of its mission to provide a broad range of information in a variety of formats, the (name of library) provides access to the Internet. Staff will conduct Internet searches when warranted as part of the library's reference and information services. Computers are also available for patrons who wish to conduct their own searches.

The library is responsible only for the information provided on its home page. Access points and links to information resources on the library's home page are selected by library staff and are checked regularly to ensure that they remain valid and consistent with the roles of the library. The library cannot monitor or control information accessed via the Internet. The library cannot guarantee that information on the Internet is accurate. If requested, staff will assist patrons in conducting searches and offer guidance on evaluating sources and verifying information.

Library staff will assist patrons with searches and suggest search strategies, but can provide limited assistance in teaching patrons how to use the Internet. The library will occasionally offer short introductory classes to familiarize patrons with the basics of Internet searching. Videotapes, books, and other learning resources are also available for patron use.

The library director will determine the Internet functions that are enabled, but generally, they will be limited to those that assist patrons in locating and obtaining information. Patrons may not initiate e-mail from library computers. Files may be downloaded to diskettes or printed to designated printers. Patrons who download files are responsible for verifying that they are free of computer viruses to protect their own computers. Charges for printing will be established on a cost-recovery basis by (governing authority). By logging on to the Internet, patrons agree to abide by the library policy on public use of microcomputers.

Parents or guardians must assume responsibility for Internet use by their children. The library will make available to parents information related to safe Internet practices. Computers in the children's room point to age-appropriate Web sites and staff is available to assist children who are conducting searches. The library will not monitor use, restrict access, or block sites. Blocking access to sites is impractical, filters out valuable information along with the potentially objectionable, and can easily be circumvented by experienced computer users.

Patrons using the Internet in the library may not display text or graphics defined by federal or state law as obscenity or pornography. Deliberate and continued display of some materials that are not obscene or pornographic may still constitute sexual harassment. Actions that violate federal, state, or local laws will be referred to the appropriate law enforcement agencies. Repeated actions that create a disturbance or that may be considered sexual harassment may result in the loss of some or all library privileges. U.S. copyright law governs unauthorized use or distribution of copyrighted materials. Users may not copy or distribute electronic materials, except as permitted by the Fair Use regulation without permission of the copyright owner.

Approved by (governing body) on (insert date)

_____

Signature of responsible representative

NOTES

1. Simpson, Carol Mann. *Copyright for School Libraries: A Practical Guide*. Worthington, OH: Linworth, 1994: 65.
2. Symons, Ann. "Kids, Sex and the Internet." *Texas Library Journal* 73, no. 2 (Summer 1997): 69.
3. Weissman, Sara K. "Do You Dare?" *members.aol.com/ saraweiss/access/index.html* (25 May 1997).
4. "Public Library Internet Access Policies." Lake Oswego (OR) Public Library. *www.ci.oswego.or.us/library/poli.htm* (25 May 1997).

5. Internet Librarianship. *www.rcls.org/libland/llinter.htm* (27 July 1997).
6. Symons, Ann. "Kids, Sex and the Internet." *Texas Library Journal* 73, no. 2 (Summer 1997): 68–72.
7. Smith, Mark. "Librarianship on the Bleeding Edge: Meeting the Pressure to Filter." *Texas Library Journal* 73, no. 2 (Summer 1997): 74–77.
8. "One Lawyer's Opinion." *Texas Library Journal* 73, no. 2 (Summer 1997): 71.
9. Montgomery-Floyd Regional Library, Internet Policy. From alaoif [discussion list], January 28, 1995.
10. "Child Safety on the Information Highway." *www.missingkids.org/childsafety.html* (25 July 1997).

Chapter 9

Access and Use of Facilities

The First Amendment to the Constitution of the United States guarantees the right to free speech. As a public institution, the library is a limited public forum for the expression of ideas. Libraries are not required to make their bulletin boards, meeting rooms, and display cases available to anyone else, but once these areas are opened to outside groups, rules and policies must be applied fairly and equitably. This can be "easier said than done" when the group wanting to use the meeting room has views that may be abhorrent to a major segment of the community. The policies presented in this chapter deal with access to and use of library spaces and facilities, including exhibit cases and decorations. Additional policies dealing with intellectual freedom can be found in Chapter 7, Collection Development, and Chapter 8, Reference and Information Services.

USE OF MEETING ROOMS

Background

In many communities, the library offers the only meeting space readily available free or at a low cost. As part of its planning and role-setting process, some libraries determine that one of the primary or secondary roles of the library will be that of Community Activities Center. That role emphasizes use of the facility as a place for community activities and meetings to occur.

Once the door to the meeting room is open to outside groups, many factors must be considered. Policies can limit times and days the meeting room is available, frequency of use, minimum and maximum size of group, charging of fees, and type of event (model policies, pages 128–129). As a public building, the library may not, and should not, be able to limit meeting content, even when the views expressed in the meeting may create conflicts within the community.

Issues

Has the library adopted the American Library Association's interpretation of the *Library Bill of Rights* that pertains to meeting rooms? Does the library want to make its meeting room available to outside groups? If not, the policy should state that the meeting room is for library use only.

Has the library selected Community Activities Center as one of its primary or secondary roles? If the library wants to make its meeting room available to the public, the policy should consider access issues to ensure fair and equitable availability of meeting space.

How frequently can a particular group schedule the meeting room? Groups meeting weekly or monthly may quickly overbook the meeting room making it difficult for those needing space on an occasional basis to find any time available. This can also make it difficult to schedule library programs. Knowing what other meeting facilities are available in the community (recreation centers, community halls, churches) will help when making decisions and provide information about alternatives for those groups that the library cannot accommodate. Examine the policies for using other community meeting room space, especially those operated by the same or related governing authority as the library.

How far in advance can groups reserve the meeting room? Allowing bookings to be made too far in advance may make it difficult to schedule library functions. On the other hand, permitting the room to be booked only a week or two in advance does not allow groups time to publicize their meetings.

Does the person booking the meeting room have to be a registered library user (have a library card)? Must the person booking the room be a resident of the service area of the library?

Will use be limited to formalized groups or can individuals and informal groups use the room? Is use limited to groups and individuals in the immediate community? Must meetings be open to the public or can private, closed meetings be held? Can admission be charged to those attending functions held in the meeting room? Can items be sold or displayed for orders to be taken? Are there any circumstances under which items or services can be sold (for example, for library or charity fundraisers)? Will for-profit groups or commercial enterprises be permitted to use the meeting room?

If the meeting or program will be advertised, it may appear that the library is co-sponsoring the event since it is being held at the library. Does library administration want to regulate wording used by organizations in their advertising or require that organizations include a statement that indicates the library does not endorse the activities?

Will library functions or meetings that further the goals of the library receive priority in scheduling?

Will a fee be charged for use of the meeting room? Who establishes the fees and will they be different for profit and non-profit groups? When, and by whom, can fees be waived?

Can refreshments be served? If refreshments are permitted, how elaborate may they be? For example, will wedding receptions or birthday parties, which usually have quite elaborate refreshments, be appropriate uses of the meeting room?

What equipment will the library provide, if any, for meetings? Can equipment be rented or borrowed from the library? If the library has erasable marker boards, consider providing the marker pens to ensure that the proper ones, which do erase, are the only ones used! Is equipment available when the library is closed and will staff be available to run the equipment? Are there limits on the type of equipment that can be brought in by those using the meeting room? (For example, can a piano be delivered for use during a program?)

Does the library have staff to arrange tables and chairs or will those using the room be responsible for moving furniture? Who is responsible for cleaning up? What happens if anything in the room is damaged or if items are missing after use? Do you want to hold a deposit that is returned after the room has been inspected?

MODEL POLICY: USE OF MEETING ROOMS, 1

A meeting room is available in the (name of library) primarily to support library programs and functions which further the goals of the library. When not being used by the library, the room is available to established not-for-profit groups based in (city, county). In accordance with the American Library Association's *Library Bill of Rights* and its interpretation pertaining to meeting rooms, the library does not limit use of the meeting room based on the subject matter or content of the meeting or on the beliefs or affiliations of the meeting's sponsors.

Except for library and library-related programs, groups may not use the meeting room more than once each month; limited series of weekly or daily meetings may be scheduled at the discretion of the library director. The meeting room may be reserved up to ninety days in advance. Fees, rules, and procedures for use of the meeting room are established by (governing authority) and are reviewed annually. A copy of the fee schedule, rules, and procedures will be provided with the application for meeting room use. A completed and signed application must be returned to the library director within two business days or the reservation may be subject to cancellation. The library director may waive fees under exceptional circumstances.

Groups using the meeting room are required to set up for their meeting, return furniture and equipment to its original location, and leave the room clean and in good condition. The library will attempt to supply standard meeting equipment, such as an overhead projector, flip chart, and chalkboard, if these items are requested when the reservation is made. However, availability of equipment cannot be guaranteed and meeting planners are encouraged to provide their own equipment. The library cannot provide consumable supplies (pens, paper).

Use of the meeting room does not imply endorsement, support, or co-sponsorship by (name of library) of the activities that take place in the meeting room or of the beliefs of the group using the meeting room. Groups or individuals using the meeting room may not imply that the event or program is sponsored, co-sponsored, or endorsed by the library in any advertising or publicity.

No selling, solicitation, or taking of orders may occur without written permission from the library director. No admission may be charged for programs held in the meeting room. Groups failing to comply with any part of this policy or the established procedures will be denied further use of the meeting room. A library staff member may be present at any time during the meeting.

Approved by (governing body) on (insert date)

_____

Signature of responsible representative

MODEL POLICY: USE OF MEETING ROOMS, 2

The library's meeting room may be used only for library related and library sponsored functions, such as children's programming, Friends of the Library meetings, and library programs. When not in use, the meeting room may be used as a quiet study room by patrons. Groups needing regular or occasional meeting space will be referred to other meeting facilities in the community.

Approved by (governing body) on (insert date)

_____

Signature of responsible representative

EXHIBITS AND DISPLAY CASES

Background

Exhibits and display cases offer members of the community the opportunity to share information, learn about hobbies, crafts, and local art, and express ideas about many things. They can provide a wonderful venue for promoting local talent, skills, and materials, and can be used to generate good public relations and increase visits to the library. Nothing brings parents into the library faster than having their child's art on display! Displays and exhibits can also be used to promote library resources and services. Libraries do not have to make their exhibit space available to anyone else, but doing so may further the library's role as a center for community activities. However, the library staff and administration do not have to endorse or advocate every viewpoint expressed in exhibits and displays. A carefully written policy will protect the library from charges of favoritism as well as from public outrage when displays offend some segment of the community.

Issues

Have you read and adopted ALA's *Library Bill of Rights* and "Exhibit Spaces and Bulletin Boards, An Interpretation of the *Library Bill of Rights*"?

What are the limitations and strengths of the library's exhibit space? Some spaces are suited for small items only. Valuable or irreplaceable items should not be displayed in a case that cannot be locked. Sculpture and three-dimensional items may not fit into shallow cases. Consider the kinds of displays that are not appropriate for your library's display case.

What function will exhibits and displays serve in meeting the overall mission of the library? Has the library selected as one of its primary roles that of Community Activities Center or Community Information Center?

Will library staff create all displays or will members of the public be able to create and set up their own displays? Must individuals or groups sponsoring an exhibit identify themselves in the exhibit? How much information must they provide (name only, or contact information also)? Will information be limited so as not to overwhelm the display case and appear to be a commercial for the organization?

Will you require that displays that focus on issues of public debate show all sides of the issue? Will the library display art that is controversial or sexually oriented?

How frequently can one individual or organization display items or create exhibits? Do you want to establish a minimum and maximum length of time each display can remain on exhibit? Too many changes will require a lot of staff time coordinating displays; too few changes make display cases stagnant and boring.

Can display and exhibit areas be secured? What types of materials can be displayed based on security needs? For example, an exhibit of sculpture might not work if the display area is out of sight from staff who could monitor the area for vandalism. Posters and other art that is not behind glass can be easily altered or vandalized.

Does the library's insurance policy cover items displayed or does the library wish to state that no liability will be accepted? Check with your legal counsel and give the information to anyone interested in exhibiting.

Will the library permit exhibits of items that are for sale? If items that are for sale (such as art, crafts, collectibles) are displayed, will sales be permitted from the display? Alternatively, will arrangements have to be made to purchase items outside of the library after the display has been dismantled?

MODEL POLICY: EXHIBITS AND DISPLAY CASES, 1

Display space is available in the library's exhibit case for educational, artistic, and cultural materials that promote interest in the use of books, library materials, and information, or that share information about local art and cultural groups. Preference will be given to exhibits that are timely and of general interest. Displays that focus on a public issue (including elections and political issues) must include information about major aspects of differing points of view. Displays that are solely commercial in focus are not appropriate.

Displays will generally be changed monthly and therefore should not be relevant for a shorter duration unless approved by the library director. Groups or individuals desiring to use the exhibit case should submit a request to the library director at least two months in advance. Generally, the same group or individual may display items one time per year.

The library director may reject any exhibit or display that does not fit with the mission of the library or that is not neat and presented attractively. Labels for exhibit items must be neat and legible.

The library will take reasonable care to ensure the safety and security of items displayed, however the library has no insurance to cover exhibit items and assumes no responsibility in the event of loss, theft, or damage. Exhibitors are encouraged to insure items of value and will be required to sign a form that releases the library from responsibility for loss, damage, or destruction. Items displayed may not include price tags or other information regarding the purchase of items. Items must be removed from the exhibit case as scheduled by the library director or they will be removed and stored for thirty days by library staff. After thirty days, they will be disposed of in accordance with local law. Display of items in the library does not indicate endorsement of the issues, events, or services promoted by those materials.

Approved by (governing body) on (insert date)

_____

Signature of responsible representative

MODEL POLICY: EXHIBITS AND DISPLAY CASES, 2

The (name of library) limits the use of its exhibit spaces to library produced exhibits. Exhibits will be prepared by library staff to reflect topics of interest or potential interest to library visitors and will present a variety of ideas on issues of contemporary interest. Library staff may borrow items from local organizations, groups, or businesses to use in the display and may credit the lender. No library space is available for unsolicited exhibits.

Approved by (governing body) on (insert date)

_____

Signature of responsible representative

DISTRIBUTION OF FREE MATERIALS

Background

Public libraries are one of the best sources of centralized local information in the community. Many other organizations, groups, and businesses want to use the library as a distribution point for their brochures, flyers, newspapers, notices, and posters. Especially if the library has determined that one of its primary or secondary roles will be that of Community Information Center, the library should encourage the display and distribution of free materials related to community events, activities, and organizations. A clear policy will help the library avoid being overwhelmed by materials and control the duration of distribution, types, formats, and size of materials distributed, and maintain order in the display rack, bulletin board, or information distribution area (model policy, pages 132–133).

The library may choose to permit only non-profit or community groups to distribute information, excluding commercial items. As a limited public forum, the library is not endorsing the content of the material displayed or distributed and should not exclude materials from groups with differing viewpoints if they meet the criteria for access to bulletin boards and information distribution areas.

Issues

Does distributing free informational materials further the library's role as a Community Information Center? Has the library board endorsed the American Library Association's interpretation of the *Library Bill of Rights* regarding exhibit space and bulletin boards?

How much information can your bulletin board or other display area(s) hold? Do you have space for flyers, brochures, newspapers, etc., to be distributed? Does staff have time to monitor and maintain bulletin board and display areas?

How do you want to limit what is distributed? Size may be a factor for bulletin boards. Also consider how long items may be posted or distributed. Will items that generally promote an organization, rather than a specific event sponsored by that organization, be distributed? Will items that promote for-profit companies, individuals, and organizations be accepted? How will political campaign materials be handled?

Will the distribution of petitions, solicitation of signatures, canvassing, or surveying of patrons be permitted on library property? Does your governing jurisdiction have laws, rules, or guidelines concerning these activities on governed property?

RELIGIOUS PROGRAMMING AND DECORATIONS

Background

Unless handled fairly and consistently, religious celebration of holidays, decorations, and programs on religion can create controversy and bad public relations. Although these issues tie in very closely with intellectual freedom, use of meeting rooms, and display of materials in the library, it may be useful to have a separate policy that addresses what is acceptable. What is acceptable and encouraged in one community may be the direct opposite of what is supported in another; it is critical to know what the community wants.

Issues

Are you aware of the religious and cultural make-up of the community served by the library? Does the library collection mirror that make-up and include information on various religious and cultural beliefs?

Does the community welcome the exploration, discussion, and

MODEL POLICY: DISTRIBUTION OF FREE MATERIALS

Items that publicize community organizations and local events further the role of the library as the central source for civic, cultural, educational, and recreational information.

Display space is available for community organizations to disseminate information. Posters and flyers displayed on the bulletin board may be no larger than 8½ inches x 14 inches. Bulletin boards may not be used for personal or commercial advertisements. Items may be displayed for a maximum of one month. Library staff will remove items that have expired or that have been posted for one month. Items removed will be discarded; library staff can not return posters and flyers that have been displayed.

Items that may be distributed include flyers, brochures, leaflets, newspapers, and pamphlets that provide information about non-profit civic, educational, cultural, or recreational organizations and events. Materials that promote programs or projects of a personal or commercial nature may not be distributed in the library. Items may be distributed for as long as they are valid. If space becomes limited, preference will be given to items of a timely nature and to organizations or groups that have not recently distributed items. Literature related to political campaigns will be distributed for thirty days preceding an election.

All items for posting or distribution must be presented to the library director for approval; library staff will date and place items on the bulletin board or in the information rack. Distribution or posting of items by the library does not indicate endorsement of the issues, events, or services promoted by those materials. Items left or posted without approval will be removed and discarded.

Approved by (governing body) on (insert date)

_____

Signature of responsible representative

celebration of diverse beliefs and do community members see the library as playing a role in encouraging diversity? Decorations and programming that reflects a wide range of beliefs may be accepted, while focusing on only one religion may not be welcome. In some communities, it is prudent to limit decorations and library sponsored programs to seasonal celebrations that reflect secular ideas (e.g., snowflakes, winter greenery, and snow characters rather than Santa Claus, Christmas trees, and crèches).

Are stories and activities presented in children's programs advertised in advance? It may be acceptable to use religious stories and holiday activities if parents know about them ahead of time so they can make decisions for their own children. Some parents may want their children to attend a storytime on Christmas but would avoid a program involving Halloween. Problems can often be prevented through advance publicity.

Does the meeting room policy state that activities conducted in the room and statements made by presenters do not necessarily indicate endorsement by the library?

MODEL POLICY: RELIGIOUS PROGRAMMING AND DECORATIONS

As part of the library's role as a Community Activities Center, the library may sponsor or present programs on a variety of topics, including holiday celebrations from various religions and cultures. Whenever possible, publicity will include details about the program so that parents may make decisions about attendance for themselves and their children. Decorations in the library, except at non-public staff desks, will be limited to secular seasonal or patriotic items, such as winter greenery, spring flowers, autumn harvest, and American flags. The library does not determine the content of programs presented by persons using the meeting room (see also the policy on "Use of Meeting Rooms"), and information presented or opinions expressed by outside speakers do not necessarily represent the views of the library.

Approved by (governing body) on (insert date)

_____

Signature of responsible representative

Chapter 10

Patron Conduct

Whether they are called patrons, customers, library users, citizens, or something else, libraries exist to serve the needs of the people who visit, call, or in some other way contact the library. Staff is in the library primarily to assist patrons, but while serving the public is generally very rewarding, it can also be aggravating, trying, and frustrating. When a court ruled for Richard Kreimer, a homeless man who had been expelled from the Morristown (NJ) Public Library, librarians panicked. They were concerned that they would no longer be able to set rules for library use or guidelines for patron behavior. An appeals court found that as limited public forums libraries could set rules necessary to ensure the orderly use of the place. The court of appeals further found that persons using the library for other than its recognized purposes could be expelled.[1] Well thought out and clearly written policies let patrons know the behaviors that are appropriate and let staff know what actions will not be tolerated. Policies also ensure that rules are reasonable and are applied consistently and fairly.

LIBRARY BEHAVIOR

Background

People who use the library have the right to facilities that are safe and comfortable to use. Safety rules and policies that expect courteous behavior and responsible actions should be enacted and enforced. While some policies may need to be directed specifically to the special situations faced by children, they should not be held to a higher standard than adults. Appropriate conduct should be expected from people of all ages. Some libraries prefer to separate the issue of unattended children left in the library from issues of behavior through separate policies. Library policy should set a tone that supports behavior that is appropriate to the services provided by the library (model policy, page 140).

Issues

Those using the library have the right to work in an environment that is conducive to its legitimate use. Are there physical factors that might interfere with having an environment that is conducive for studying, reading, and research?

Rules of conduct should be made with the interests of patrons foremost in mind. Consider the library layout before imposing unnecessarily restrictive rules. For example, cellular phones, personal pagers, laptop computers, and portable typewriters, even the quietest of which make some noise, may be permitted in a general reading area, but not in quiet study areas. Personal audio devices with headphones may be used almost anywhere without disturbing others. If quiet study carrels are readily available, low-toned conversations may be permissible in general areas. Will the library's electrical system and layout permit the use of personal appliances? Older buildings and buildings with inadequate power supplies may not be able to handle additional appliances. In addition, patrons might remove the plugs for library appliances in order to plug in their own devices.

All patrons, regardless of age, should be expected to follow the same rules of conduct. Children may require additional consideration because of their youth and vulnerability, but should not be held to a higher standard of conduct than is expected of adults. Staff should not be expected to be babysitters for children left unattended. If this is a particular problem in your community, consider having a separate policy on unattended children or children left in the library after closing (see policy on "Unattended Children").

Staff should not be subjected to abusive language and inappropriate behavior from patrons. Has staff been trained to respond coolly to anger? Have procedures been established so that staff may remove themselves from abusive situations?

Policy should address general areas of behavior and be broad enough to include actions or behaviors not mentioned. Do not attempt to list every conceivable negative action or inappropriate behavior. A determined patron can always find something to do that you will not have considered!

Do you know what local law enforcement agency will respond to calls for assistance? Have you discussed the parameters of legal enforcement? Do you have a commitment for support from that agency?

UNATTENDED CHILDREN

Background

The primary concern regarding underage children who are left unattended in the library must be for their safety. Preschool children should never be unsupervised and it is the opinion of many librarians that to do so constitutes child neglect. Children who are old enough to be in the library on their own are often called "latchkey" children. They may be sent to the library after school until a working parent can pick them up, or they may prefer being in the library to being home alone. These children should be subject to the same guidelines for patron behavior as adults and not be treated differently just because of their age. An additional problem may occur with children who are old enough to be in the library alone, but are unable to get home on their own and are still at the library at closing time (model policy, page 142).

Issues

Any policy must address concern for the safety and well-being of children. Additional concerns are for maintaining an orderly place where all patrons can make appropriate use of the library.

What is the age in your community under which children may not be left without adult supervision? The age under which a child can be considered abandoned if left without parental or other adult supervision is generally established by the legal system.

What other facilities are there for child care in the community?

MODEL POLICY: LIBRARY BEHAVIOR

The (name of library) encourages people of all ages to visit the library. Those using the library and its resources have the right to expect a safe, comfortable environment that supports appropriate library services.

People demonstrating disruptive behavior will be required to leave the library after one warning from library staff. Disruptive behavior includes, but is not limited to, noisy, boisterous actions; inappropriate behavior, including eating, smoking, running, or loud talking; misuse of library property; uncooperative attitude; or actions that deliberately annoy others or prevent the legitimate use of the library and its resources. Abusive language and behavior toward staff will not be tolerated.

Personal appliances, such as computers, cassette players, and calculators, may be used if the noise level is low and use does not interfere with others. Because of the lack of outlets and concern for electrical overload, all appliances must be battery-powered and may not be plugged into library outlets. Portable telephones and pagers should be turned off or switched to a non-audible signal and should be answered outside the library.

Young children are not safe when left unattended in the library. Staff cannot know if children are leaving with a parent, a friend, or a stranger. Library staff will not deliberately seek out unattended children; however, unattended children frequently become disruptive when they become bored. Parents are responsible for ensuring the appropriate behavior of their children while in the library. If a parent or other responsible adult cannot be located, unattended children who are disruptive will be placed in the care of (specify local law enforcement officials). Under no circumstances will library staff take a child out of the building or transport children to another location.

Approved by (governing body) on (insert date)

_____

Signature of responsible representative

Problems with unattended children are better resolved by offering solutions for parents who may feel they have no other choices for their children. The Public Library Association's Service to Children Committee implores libraries to be involved in finding solutions to a community-wide problem and suggests that the library serve as a catalyst for change.

Have you discussed concerns about the safety of children and appropriate actions with the local law enforcement authorities? Support from law enforcement authorities will allow the library to establish policies and write procedures that will be enforceable. Without support, the library runs the risk of receiving no response or getting an inappropriate response from law enforcement agents who may feel that the library is unnecessarily calling on them.

Have you discussed liability for unattended children with your legal counsel? Although the public library does not have the same provision of care responsibilities that schools and child care centers have, local laws may set stricter standards. Under no circumstances is it advisable for library staff to transport children in a personal vehicle. Especially in small, close-knit communities, this can be an uncomfortable, but necessary part of the policy.

Are parents leaving young children in the library while they run other errands? Some parents assume that the library is a safe haven for their children and will drop young children off for programs while they leave for a short time. Are signs posted warning parents not to leave the building while their children are in library-sponsored programs? Are brochures available that explain concern for the safety of children left unattended? If possible, brochures should also offer suggestions for alternatives to leaving a child alone in the library.

Is the library within walking distance of most households in the community or near public transportation? Are library hours clearly posted and kept as consistent as possible so that parents know when the library closes? Children should never be left waiting outside alone after all staff members have left the building.

MODEL POLICY: UNATTENDED CHILDREN

The (name of library) is a public facility that offers services to a wide range of citizens, and children are especially welcome. The library has the responsibility to provide an environment that is safe and comfortable for every patron who is appropriately using its services and facilities. Children and young people are expected to adhere to the same standards of patron conduct expected of adults. Parents, guardians, or assigned chaperones are responsible for the behavior of their children while in the library.

Children under the age of seven should *never* be left unsupervised in any area of the library. If a parent cannot be located, staff will call the (proper authorities) to report an abandoned child.

Older children who are disruptive will be asked to leave the library (see policy on "Library Behavior"). If the child cannot safely leave the library to return home on his or her own, staff will permit the child to call a parent. If no parent can be contacted, library staff will either allow the child to remain at the library under close supervision until a parent can be contacted or contact the (proper authorities), depending upon the severity of the situation.

Children who have not been picked up at closing time will be given the opportunity to call a parent. Children who have not been picked up within fifteen minutes after closing will be left in the care of (proper authorities). Under no circumstances will staff transport children in a vehicle or accompany them home.

Approved by (governing body) on (insert date)

_____

Signature of responsible representative

HARASSMENT AND LEWD BEHAVIOR

Background

It is understood that patrons and staff should be able to work in an environment free from sexual harassment, lewd behavior, or other forms of harassment. It is important that the library respond to any allegations of harassment, especially sexual harassment, including those involving two patrons or a patron and a staff member. A policy on harassment, and immediate action in response to complaints of inappropriate behavior, will reduce the likelihood of a lawsuit against the library and its governing authority.

Issues

Has staff received training to recognize and respond to sexual harassment? Has staff been instructed how to respond to complaints from patrons about lewd behavior or other types of harassment? All complaints should be taken seriously and staff should thank library users, especially children, for reporting all incidents.

Do you know what law enforcement agency to contact to report serious incidents of lewd conduct? Serious incidents include any incidents involving an unwilling person, inappropriate or indecent behavior with a child, and continued behavior that makes another person unable to continue using the library. Minor incidents, such as teenagers making out in the library or name-calling may be handled as inappropriate behavior unless problems persist.

Does the library's governing authority have a policy prohibiting sexual harassment? To what office or agency are incidents to be reported? Does staff know the process for reporting incidents of harassment?

Must a staff member have observed the incident in order to call law enforcement? Some jurisdictions require that the person involved or a witness file the complaint. Check with your legal counsel!

Any incident involving a child should be reported to the child's parent, who should also be informed of any action taken by the library.

MODEL POLICY: HARASSMENT AND LEWD BEHAVIOR

Patrons and staff have the right to enjoy an environment free from harassment or lewd conduct. Anyone, including patrons, who harasses staff or another patron will be asked to leave the library and a report will be filed with the director. Repeated acts of harassment or acts that may escalate into violent or illegal actions will be reported to (proper authorities).

Lewd acts or sexual misconduct is not appropriate in the library. Those who commit minor acts, such as teenagers who "make out" in the library, will be given one warning and then asked to leave. Serious acts and acts involving minors will be reported to (proper authorities). All serious acts will be reported to the director.

Approved by (governing body) on (insert date)

——————————————————————

Signature of responsible representative

PATRON USE OF LIBRARY SUPPLIES

Background

Patrons are expected to bring common office supplies (e.g., paper, pens, paper clips, index cards) they need with them. Libraries with public-access computers are also frequently asked to supply diskettes for downloading files. Supply budgets are limited and these materials are generally consumable or, if they are borrowed for use, may not be returned. However, in the interest of customer service, libraries frequently provide scratch paper (usually recycled from the photocopier or left over from other projects) and pencils for use at the card or online catalog. Libraries may also provide paper cutters, scissors, staplers, or other materials for use at the photocopier.

Consider the public relations value of supplying some items, versus the nuisance factor of having to justify not loaning a pencil or providing a paper clip to a patron. It is helpful to have some pencils available for loan if the library serves students and children, especially if the library has selected Formal Education Support Center as one of its primary or secondary roles. Some libraries

Center as one of its primary or secondary roles. Some libraries choose to have small quantities of paper, envelopes, pens, correction fluid, etc., available for purchase at cost or to generate small amounts of revenue for the library.

Issues

What supplies can be provided without cost, at low cost, or without affecting the library supply budget? Would a stapler and similar equipment aid those who use the photocopier?

Does the library wish to resell small quantities of common supplies? Does the library's governing authority permit revolving accounts to allow the purchase of additional items for sale from the funds collected? Who will collect the money? How will supplies be replenished? Is there a library store or gift shop that could sell office supplies?

Are there stores nearby that sell paper, pens, and other office supplies? How inconvenient will it be for someone to have to run out to purchase index cards, diskettes, correction fluid, etc.?

MODEL POLICY: PATRON USE OF LIBRARY SUPPLIES

The (name of library) supplies scratch paper, recycled from the photocopier and other sources, for note taking but cannot provide other office or school supplies. Office supplies purchased with library budget funds are for use by the library staff in the completion of their work. Because they are purchased with public tax funds, they cannot be sold or given away. Small quantities of typing paper, pens, index cards, computer diskettes, etc., are available for purchase at the circulation desk priced on a cost-recovery basis.

Approved by (governing body) on (insert date)

_____

Signature of responsible representative

THEFT OF MATERIALS

Background

Libraries lose items to theft; it is a part of doing business and a clever and determined thief will overcome any security or theft detection system. The challenge is to reduce theft without creating an armed camp where legitimate library users feel that they are under constant surveillance and considered guilty unless proven innocent. Policies should be written so that everyone is subject to the same inconvenience or questioning. Remember that this type of policy must be reasonable and must be applied fairly and consistently. Even the appearance that only some people are subject to the policy could result in adverse legal action. If personal items are to be examined, signs should be posted alerting patrons that items brought into the library are subject to search. It is probably better to err on the side of losing a few items, rather than to become the "library police."

Issues

Do you know what percentage of the library collection is lost to theft each year? Do you have a theft detection system? How reliable is it? What is the frequency of false alarms? Has staff been adequately trained in the methods of desensitizing tags?

Do you want to examine books, bookbags, briefcases, backpacks, and other containers as they leave the library? Do you have staff to handle this function? Are signs posted to inform people that their belongings may be searched as they leave the library?

Does the library have security staff who can monitor patrons coming in and exiting the library? If not, is staff comfortable with this responsibility? Staff should not confront aggressive or agitated persons and should receive training on how to deal with people who are angry, emotionally disturbed, or threatening.

Do you want to exclude suitcases, bedrolls, duffel bags, and other large bags from being brought into the library? Is there a place where these items can be safely stored while the owner is using the library? Take care that excluding these items from the library does not act also to exclude the owner. Caution is especially important if items will be stored at the circulation desk. Staff should not be subjected to charges of pilfering or held responsible for monitoring personal items.

Have you discussed your plans with your legal counsel? Are you familiar with any laws or local ordinances that deal with the search of an individual's property?

MODEL POLICY: THEFT OF MATERIALS

To protect the investment in library materials made by taxpayers, as patrons leave the library, staff may conduct random examinations of bookbags, backpacks, briefcases, and other large containers brought into the library. Any uncharged items will be returned to the circulation desk to be charged out. If staff believes that, due to the large volume of materials and/or value of materials, theft was intended, the police will be immediately notified. Vandalism of library materials will also be reported to the police.

Signs indicating that personal items may be examined will be posted at the entrance and inside the library. Storage lockers are provided at no charge for library patrons not wishing to have their personal items be subject to search. Bedrolls, duffel bags, suitcases, and other large tote bags must be stored in the lockers or checked at the front desk, but may not be brought into the library. The library will exercise caution with items stored at the desk but cannot assume responsibility for loss or theft.

Approved by (governing body) on (insert date)

_____

Signature of responsible representative

NOTE

1. Bielefield, Arlene and Lawrence Cheeseman. *Library Patrons and the Law*. New York: Neal-Schuman, 1995, pp. 93–94.

Appendix A

Codes of Ethics

AMERICAN LIBRARY ASSOCIATION CODE OF ETHICS

As members of the American Library Association, we recognize the importance of codifying and making known to the profession and to the general public the ethical principles that guide the work of librarians, other professionals providing information services, library trustees and library staffs.

Ethical dilemmas occur when values are in conflict. The American Library Association Code of Ethics states the values to which we are committed, and embodies the ethical responsibilities of the profession in this changing information environment.

We significantly influence or control the selection, organization, preservation, and dissemination of information. In a political system grounded in an informed citizenry, we are members of a profession explicitly committed to intellectual freedom and the freedom of access to information. We have a special obligation to ensure the free flow of information and ideas to present and future generations.

The principles of this Code are expressed in broad statements to guide ethical decision making. These statements provide a framework; they cannot and do not dictate conduct to cover particular situations.

I. We provide the highest level of service to all library users through appropriate and usefully organized resources; equitable service policies; equitable access; and accurate, unbiased, and courteous responses to all requests.

II. We uphold the principles of intellectual freedom and resist all efforts to censor library resources.

III. We protect each library user's right to privacy and confidentially with respect to information sought or received and resources consulted, borrowed, acquired, or transmitted.

IV. We recognize and respect intellectual property rights.

V. We treat co-worker and other colleagues with respect, fairness and good faith, and advocate conditions of employment that safeguard the rights and welfare of all employees of our institutions.

VI. We do not advance private interests at the expense of library users, colleagues, or our employing institutions.

VII. We distinguish between our personal convictions and professional duties and do not allow our personal beliefs to interfere with fair representation of the aims of our institutions or the provision of access to their information resources.

VIII. We strive for excellence in the profession by maintaining and enhancing our own knowledge and skills, by encouraging the professional development of co-workers, and by fostering the aspirations of potential members of the profession.

Adopted by ALA Council, June 1995

ETHICS STATEMENT FOR PUBLIC LIBRARY TRUSTEES

Trustees must promote a high level of library service while observing ethical standards.

Trustees must avoid situations in which personal interests might be served or financial benefits gained at the expense of library users, colleagues, or the institution.

It is incumbent upon any trustee to disqualify himself/herself immediately whenever the appearance of a conflict of interest exists.

Trustees must distinguish clearly in their actions and statements between their personal philosophies and attitudes and those of the institution, acknowledging the formal position of the board even if they personally disagree.

A trustee must respect the confidential nature of library business while being aware of and in compliance with applicable laws governing freedom of information.

Trustees must be prepared to support to the fullest the efforts of librarians in resisting censorship of library materials by groups or individuals.

Trustees who accept appointment to a library board are expected to perform all of the functions of library trustees.

Approved by the PLA Board of Directors, July 8, 1985; approved by the ALTA Board of Directors, July 8, 1985.

Appendix B

Guidelines for the Development and Implementation of Policies, Regulations, and Procedures Affecting Access to Library Materials, Services, and Facilities

INTRODUCTION

Publicly supported libraries exist within the context of a body of law derived from the United States Constitution and appropriate state constitutions, defined by statute, and implemented by regulations, policies, and procedures established by their governing bodies and administrations. These regulations, policies, and procedures establish the mission of the library, define its functions, services, and operations and ascertain the rights and responsibilities of the clientele served by the library.

Publicly supported library service is based upon the First Amendment right of free expression. The publicly supported library provides free and equal access to information for all people of the community it serves. Thus, publicly supported libraries are governmental agencies designated as limited public forums for access to information. Libraries that make meeting rooms, exhibit spaces, and/or bulletin boards available for public use are also designated as limited public forums for the exchange of information.

Many libraries adopt administrative policies and procedures regulating the organization and use of library materials, services, and facilities. These policies and procedures affect access and may have the effect of restricting, denying, or creating barriers to access to the library as a public forum, including the library's resources, facilities, and services. Library policies and procedures that impinge upon First Amendment rights are subject to a higher standard of review than may be required in the policies of other public services and facilities.

Policies, procedures, or regulations that may result in denying, restricting, or creating physical or economic barriers to access to the library's public forum must be based on a compelling government interest. However, library governing authorities may place reasonable and narrowly drawn restrictions on the time, place, or manner of access to library resources, services, or facilities, provided that such restrictions are not based upon arbitrary distinctions between individuals or classes of individuals.

The American Library Association has adopted the *Library Bill of Rights* and "Interpretations of the Library Bill of Rights" to provide library governing authorities, librarians, and other library staff and library users with guidelines on how constitutional principles apply to libraries in the United States of America.

The American Library Association's Intellectual Freedom Committee recommends that publicly supported libraries use the following guidelines, based on constitutional principles, to develop policies, regulations, and procedures.

GUIDELINES

All library policies, regulations, and procedures should be carefully examined to determine if they may result in denying, restricting, or creating barriers to access. If they may result in such restrictions, they:

1. should be developed and implemented within the legal framework that applies to the library. This includes: the United States Constitution, including the First and Fourteenth Amendments, due process and equal treatment under the law; the applicable state constitution; federal and state civil rights

legislation; all other applicable federal, state, and local legislation; and applicable case law;

2. should cite statutes or ordinances upon which the authority to make that policy is based, when appropriate;

3. should be developed and implemented within the framework of the Library Bill of Rights and its Interpretations;

4. should be based upon the library's mission and objectives;

5. should only impose restrictions on the access to, or use of library resources, services, or facilities when those restrictions are necessary to achieve the library's mission and objectives;

6. should narrowly tailor prohibitions or restrictions, in the rare instances when they are required, so they are not more restrictive than needed to serve their objectives;

7. should attempt to balance competing interests and avoid favoring the majority at the expense of individual rights, or allowing individual users' rights to interfere materially with the majority's rights to free and equal access to library resources, services, and facilities;

8. should avoid arbitrary distinctions between individuals or classes of users, and should not have the effect of denying or abridging a person's right to use library resources, services, or facilities based upon arbitrary distinctions such as origin, age, background, or views;

In the *Library Bill of Rights* and all of its Interpretations, it is intended that: "origin" encompasses all the characteristics of individuals that are inherent in the circumstances of their birth; "age" encompasses all the characteristics of individuals that are inherent in their levels of development and maturity; "background" encompasses all the characteristics of individuals that are a result of their life experiences; and "views" encompasses all the opinions and beliefs held and expressed by individuals;

9. should not target specific users or groups of users based upon an assumption or expectation that such users might engage in behavior that will materially interfere with the achievement of substantial library objectives;

10. must be clearly stated so that a reasonably intelligent person will have fair warning of what is expected;
11. must provide a means of appeal;
12. must be reviewed regularly by the library's governing authority and by its legal counsel.
13. must be communicated clearly and made available in an effective manner to all library users;
14. must be enforced evenhandedly, and not in a manner intended to benefit or disfavor any person or group in an arbitrary or capricious manner;

Libraries should develop an ongoing staff training program designed to foster the understanding of the legal framework and principles underlying library policies and to assist staff in gaining the skill and ability to respond to potentially difficult circumstances in a timely, direct, and open manner. This program should include training to develop empathy and understanding of the social and economic problems of some library users; and

15. should, if reasonably possible, provide adequate alternative means of access to information for those whose behavior results in the denial or restriction of access to any library resource, service, or facility.

Adopted by the ALA Intellectual Freedom Committee, June 28, 1994.

Library Bill of Rights and Interpretations of the Library Bill of Rights

THE LIBRARY BILL OF RIGHTS

The American Library Association affirms that all libraries are forums for information and ideas, and that the following basic policies should guide their services.

1. Books and other library resources should be provided for the interest, information, and enlightenment of all people of the community the library serves. Materials should not be excluded because of the origin, background, or views of those contributing to their creation.

2. Libraries should provide materials and information presenting all points of view on current and historical issues. Materials should not be proscribed or removed because of partisan or doctrinal disapproval.

3. Libraries should challenge censorship in the fulfillment of their responsibility to provide information and enlightenment.

4. Libraries should cooperate with all persons and groups concerned with resisting abridgment of free expression and free access to ideas.

5. A person's right to use a library should not be denied or abridged because of origin, age, background, or views.

6. Libraries which make exhibit spaces and meeting rooms available to the public they serve should make such facilities available on an equitable basis, regardless of the beliefs or affiliations of individuals or groups requesting their use.

Adopted June 18, 1948; amended February 2, 1961, and January 23, 1980, by the ALA Council.

STATEMENT ON LABELING: AN INTERPRETATION OF THE *LIBRARY BILL OF RIGHTS*

Labeling is the practice of describing or designating materials by affixing a prejudicial label and/or segregating them by a prejudicial system. The American Library Association opposes these means of predisposing people's attitudes toward library materials for the following reasons:

1. Labeling is an attempt to prejudice attitudes and as such, it is a censor's tool.
2. Some find it easy and even proper, according to their ethics, to establish criteria for judging publications as objectionable. However, injustice and ignorance rather than justice and enlightenment result from such practices, and the American Library Association opposes the establishment of such criteria.
3. Libraries do not advocate the ideas found in their collections. The presence of books and other resources in a library does not indicate endorsement of their contents by the library.

A variety of private organizations promulgate rating systems and/ or review materials as a means of advising either their members or the general public concerning their opinions of the contents and suitability or appropriate age for use of certain books, films, recordings, or other materials. For the library to adopt or enforce any of these private systems, to attach such ratings to library materials, to include them in bibliographic records, library catalogs, or other finding aids, or otherwise to endorse them would violate the *Library Bill of Rights*.

While some attempts have been made to adopt these systems into law, the constitutionality of such measures is extremely questionable. If such legislation is passed which applies within a library's jurisdiction, the library should seek competent legal advice concerning its applicability to library operations.

Publishers, industry groups, and distributors sometimes add ratings to material or include them as part of their packaging. Librarians should not endorse such practices. However, removing or obliterating such ratings—if placed there by or with permission of the copyright holder—could constitute expurgation, which is also unacceptable.

The American Library Association opposes efforts which aim at closing any path to knowledge. This statement, however, does not exclude the adoption of organizational schemes designed as directional aids or to facilitate access to materials.

Adopted July 13, 1951. Amended June 25, 1971; July 1, 1981; June 26, 1990, by the ALA Council.

CHALLENGED MATERIALS: AN INTERPRETATION OF THE *LIBRARY BILL OF RIGHTS*

The American Library Association declares as a matter of firm principle that it is the responsibility of every library to have a clearly defined materials selection policy in written form that reflects the *Library Bill of Rights*, and that is approved by the appropriate governing authority.

Challenged materials that meet the criteria for selection in the materials selection policy of the library should not be removed under any legal or extra-legal pressure. The *Library Bill of Rights* states in Article I that "Materials should not be excluded because of the origin, background, or views of those contributing to their creation," and in Article II, that "Materials should not be proscribed or removed because of partisan or doctrinal disapproval." Freedom of expression is protected by the Constitution of the United States, but constitutionally protected expression is often separated from unprotected expression only by a dim and uncertain line. The Constitution requires a procedure designed to focus searchingly on challenged expression before it can be suppressed. An adversary hearing is a part of this procedure. Therefore, any attempt, be it legal or extra-legal, to regulate or suppress materials in libraries must be closely scrutinized to the end that protected expression is not abridged.

Adopted June 25, 1971; amended July 1, 1981; amended January 10, 1990, by the ALA Council

FREE ACCESS TO LIBRARIES FOR MINORS: AN INTERPRETATION OF THE *LIBRARY BILL OF RIGHTS*

Library policies and procedures that effectively deny minors equal access to all library resources available to other users violate the *Library Bill of Rights*. The American Library Association opposes all attempts to restrict access to library services, materials, and facilities based on the age of library users.

Article V of the *Library Bill of Rights* states, "A person's right to use a library should not be denied or abridged because of origin, age, background, or views." The "right to use a library" includes free access to, and unrestricted use of, all the services, materials, and facilities the library has to offer. Every restriction on access to, and use of, library resources, based solely on the chronological age, educational level, or legal emancipation of users violates Article V.

Libraries are charged with the mission of developing resources to meet the diverse information needs and interests of the communities they serve. Services, materials, and facilities that fulfill the needs and interests of library users at different stages in their personal development are a necessary part of library resources. The needs and interests of each library user, and resources appropriate to meet those needs and interests, must be determined on an individual basis. Librarians cannot predict what resources will best fulfill the needs and interests of any individual user based on a single criterion such as chronological age, level of education, or legal emancipation.

The selection and development of library resources should not be diluted because of minors having the same access to library resources as adult users. Institutional self-censorship diminishes the credibility of the library in the community, and restricts access for all library users.

Librarians and governing bodies should not resort to age restrictions on access to library resources in an effort to avoid actual or anticipated objections from parents or anyone else. The mission, goals, and objectives of libraries do not authorize librarians or governing bodies to assume, abrogate, or overrule the rights and responsibilities of parents or legal guardians. Librarians and governing bodies should maintain that parents—and only parents—have the right and the responsibility to restrict the access of their children—and only their children—to library resources. Parents or legal guardians who do not want their children to have access to certain library services, materials, or facilities should so advise their children. Librarians and governing bodies cannot assume the role of parents or the functions of parental authority in the private relationship between parent and child. Librarians and governing bodies have a public and professional obligation to provide equal access to all library resources for all library users.

Librarians have a professional commitment to ensure that all members of the community they serve have free and equal access to the entire range of library resources regardless of content, approach, format, or amount of detail. This principle of library service applies equally to all users, minors as well as adults. Librarians and governing bodies must uphold this principle in order to provide adequate and effective service to minors.

Adopted June 30, 1972; amended July 1, 1981; July 3, 1991, by the ALA Council.

LIBRARY INITIATED PROGRAMS AS A RESOURCE: AN INTERPRETATION OF THE *LIBRARY BILL OF RIGHTS*

Library initiated programs support the mission of the library by providing users with additional opportunities for information, education, and recreation. Article 1 of the *Library Bill of Rights* states: "Books and other library resources should be provided for the interest, information and enlightenment of all people of the community the library serves."

Library initiated programs take advantage of library staff expertise, collections, services, and facilities to increase access to information and information resources. Library initiated programs introduce users and potential users to the resources of the library and to the library's primary function as a facilitator of information access. The library may participate in cooperative or joint programs with other agencies, organizations, institutions, or individuals as part of its own effort to address information needs and to facilitate information access in the community the library serves.

Library initiated programs on site and in other locations include, but are not limited to, speeches, community forums, discussion groups, demonstrations, displays, and live or media presentations.

Libraries serving multilingual or multicultural communities make efforts to accommodate the information needs of those for whom English is a second language. Library initiated programs across language and cultural barriers introduce otherwise unserved populations to the resources of the library and provide access to information.

Library initiated programs "should not be proscribed or removed (or canceled) because of partisan or doctrinal disapproval" of the contents of the program or the views expressed by the participants, as stated in Article 2 of the *Library Bill of Rights*. Library sponsorship of a program does not constitute an endorsement of the content of the program or the views expressed by the participants, any more than the purchase of material for the library collection constitutes an endorsement of the contents of the material or the views of its creator.

Library staff select topics, speakers, and resource materials for library initiated programs based on the interests and information needs of the community. Topics, speakers, and resource materials are not excluded from library initiated programs because of possible controversy. Concerns, questions, or complaints about library initiated programs are handled according to the same written policy and procedures that govern reconsiderations of other library resources.

Library initiated programs are offered free of charge and are open to all. Article 5 of the *Library Bill of Rights* states: "A person's right to use a library should not be denied or abridged because of origin, age, background, or views."

The "right to use a library" encompasses all of the resources the library offers, including the right to attend library initiated programs. Libraries do not deny or abridge access to library resources, including library initiated programs, based on an individual's economic background and ability to pay.

Adopted January 27, 1982. Amended June 26, 1990, by the ALA Council.

DIVERSITY IN COLLECTION DEVELOPMENT: AN INTERPRETATION OF THE *LIBRARY BILL OF RIGHTS*

Throughout history, the focus of censorship has fluctuated from generation to generation. Books and other materials have not been selected or have been removed from library collections for many reasons, among which are prejudicial language and ideas, political content, economic theory, social philosophies, religious beliefs, sexual forms of expression, and other topics of a potentially controversial nature.

Some examples of censorship may include removing or not selecting materials because they are considered by some as racist or sexist; not purchasing conservative religious materials; not selecting materials about or by minorities because it is thought these groups or interests are not represented in a community; or not providing information on or materials from non-mainstream political entities.

Librarians may seek to increase user awareness of materials on various social concerns by many means, including, but not limited to, issuing bibliographies and presenting exhibits and programs.

Librarians have a professional responsibility to be inclusive, not exclusive, in collection development and in the provision of interlibrary loan. Access to all materials legally obtainable should be assured to the user, and policies should not unjustly exclude materials even if they are offensive to the librarian or the user. Collection development should reflect the philosophy inherent in Article 2 of the *Library Bill of Rights*: "Libraries should provide materials and information presenting all points of view on current and historical issues. Materials should not be proscribed or removed because of partisan or doctrinal disapproval." A balanced collection reflects a diversity of responsibilities including selecting materials in the languages in common use in the community that the library serves. Collection development and the selection of materials should be done according to professional standards and established selection and review procedures.

There are many complex facets to any issue, and variations of context in which issues may be expressed, discussed, or interpreted. Librarians have a professional responsibility to be fair, just, and equitable and to give all library users equal protection in guarding against violation of the library patron's right to read, view, or listen to materials and resources protected by the First Amendment, no matter what viewpoint of the author, creator, or selector. Librarians have an obligation to protect library collections from removal of materials based on personal bias or prejudice, and to select and support the access to materials on all subjects that meet, as closely as possible, the needs and interests of all persons in the community that the library serves. This includes materials that reflect political, economic, religious, social, minority, and sexual issues.

Intellectual freedom, the essence of equitable library services, provides for free access to all expressions of ideas through which any and all sides of a question, cause, or movement may be explored. Toleration is meaningless without tolerance for what some may consider detestable. Librarians cannot justly permit their own preferences to limit their degree of tolerance in collection development, because freedom is indivisible.

Adopted July 14, 1982; amended January 10, 1990, by the ALA Council.

ACCESS FOR CHILDREN AND YOUNG PEOPLE TO VIDEOTAPES AND OTHER NON-PRINT FORMATS: AN INTERPRETATION OF THE *LIBRARY BILL OF RIGHTS*

Library collections of videotapes, motion pictures, and other non-print formats raise a number of intellectual freedom issues, especially regarding minors.

The interests of young people, like those of adults, are not limited by subject, theme, or level of sophistication. Librarians have a responsibility to ensure young people have access to materials and services that reflect diversity sufficient to meet their needs.

To guide librarians and others in resolving these issues, the American Library Association provides the following guidelines.

Article V of the *Library Bill of Rights* says, "A person's right to use a library should not be denied or abridged because of origin, age, background, or views."

ALA's "Free Access to Libraries for Minors: An Interpretation of the *Library Bill of Rights*" states: The "right to use a library" includes free access to, and unrestricted use of, all the services, materials, and facilities the library has to offer. Every restriction on access to, and use of, library resources, based solely on the chronological age, educational level, or legal emancipation of users violates Article V.

Parents—and only parents—have the right and the responsibility to restrict the access of their children—and only their children— to library resources. Parents or legal guardians who do not want their children to have access to certain library services, materials, or facilities should so advise their children. Librarians and governing bodies cannot assume the role of parents or the functions of parental authority in the private relationship between parent and child. Librarians and governing bodies have a public and professional obligation to provide equal access to all library resources for all library users.

Policies that set minimum age limits for access to videotapes and/or other audiovisual materials and equipment, with or without parental permission, abridge library use for minors. Further, age limits based on the cost of materials are unacceptable. Unless directly and specifically prohibited by law from circulating certain motion pictures and video productions to minors, librarians should apply the same standards to circulation of these materials as are applied to books and other materials.

Recognizing that libraries cannot act in loco parentis, ALA acknowledges and supports the exercise by parents of their responsibility to guide their own children's reading and viewing. Published reviews of films and videotapes and/or reference works that provide information about the content, subject matter, and recommended audiences can be made available in conjunction with non-print collections to assist parents in guiding their children without implicating the library in censorship. This material may include information provided by video producers and distributors, promotional material on videotape packaging, and Motion Picture Association of America (MPAA) ratings if they are included on the tape or in the packaging by the original publisher and/or if they appear in review sources or reference works included in the library's collection. Marking out or removing ratings information from videotape packages constitutes expurgation or censorship.

MPAA and other rating services are private advisory codes and have no legal standing.* For the library to add such ratings to the materials if they are not already there, to post a list of such ratings with a collection, or to attempt to enforce such ratings through circulation policies or other procedures constitutes labeling, "an attempt to prejudice attitudes" about the material, and is unacceptable. The application of locally generated ratings schemes intended to provide content warnings to library users is also inconsistent with the *Library Bill of Rights*.

Adopted June 28, 1989, by the ALA Council; the quotation from "Free Access to Libraries for Minors" was changed after Council adopted the July 3, 1991, revision of that Interpretation.

---

*For information on case law, please contact the ALA Office for Intellectual Freedom. See also: "Statement on Labeling" and "Expurgation of Library Materials, Interpretations of the *Library Bill of Rights*."

MEETING ROOMS: AN INTERPRETATION OF THE
LIBRARY BILL OF RIGHTS

Many libraries provide meeting rooms for individuals and groups as part of a program of service. Article VI of the *Library Bill of Rights* states that such facilities should be made available to the public served by the given library "on an equitable basis, regardless of the beliefs or affiliations of individuals or groups requesting their use."

Libraries maintaining meeting room facilities should develop and publish policy statements governing use. These statements can properly define time, place, or manner of use; such qualifications should not pertain to the content of a meeting or to the beliefs or affiliations of the sponsors. These statements should be made available in any commonly used language within the community served.

If meeting rooms in libraries supported by public funds are made available to the general public for non-library sponsored events, the library may not exclude any group based on the subject matter to be discussed or based on the ideas that the group advocates. For example, if a library allows charities and sports clubs to discuss their activities in library meeting rooms, then the library should not exclude partisan political or religious groups from discussing their activities in the same facilities. If a library opens its meeting rooms to a wide variety of civic organizations, then the library may not deny access to a religious organization. Libraries may wish to post a permanent notice near the meeting room stating that the library does not advocate or endorse the viewpoints of meetings or meeting room users.

Written policies for meeting room use should be stated in inclusive rather than exclusive terms. For example, a policy that the library's facilities are open "to organizations engaged in educational, cultural, intellectual, or charitable activities" is an inclusive statement of the limited uses to which the facilities may be put. This defined limitation would permit religious groups to use the facilities because they engage in intellectual activities, but would exclude most commercial uses of the facility.

A publicly supported library may limit use of its meeting rooms to strictly "library-related" activities, provided that the limitation is clearly circumscribed and is viewpoint neutral. Written policies may include limitations on frequency of use, and whether or not meetings held in library meeting rooms must be open to the public. If state and local laws permit private as well as public sessions of meetings in libraries, libraries may choose to offer both options. The same standard should be applicable to all.

If meetings are open to the public, libraries should include in their meeting room policy statement a section that addresses admission fees. If admission fees are permitted, libraries shall seek to make it possible that these fees do not limit access to individuals who may be unable to pay, but who wish to attend the meeting. Article V of the *Library Bill of Rights* states that "a person's right to use a library should not be denied or abridged because of origin, age, background, or views." It is inconsistent with Article V to restrict indirectly access to library meeting rooms based on an individual's or group's ability to pay for that access.

Adopted July 2, 1991, by the ALA Council.

EXHIBIT SPACES AND BULLETIN BOARDS: AN INTERPRETATION OF THE *LIBRARY BILL OF RIGHTS*

Libraries often provide exhibit spaces and bulletin boards. The uses made of these spaces should conform to the *Library Bill of Rights*: Article I states, "Materials should not be excluded because of the origin, background, or views of those contributing to their creation." Article II states, "Materials should not be proscribed or removed because of partisan or doctrinal disapproval." Article VI maintains that exhibit space should be made available "on an equitable basis, regardless of the beliefs or affiliations of individuals or groups requesting their use."

In developing library exhibits, staff members should endeavor to present a broad spectrum of opinion and a variety of viewpoints. Libraries should not shrink from developing exhibits because of controversial content or because of the beliefs or affiliations of those whose work is represented. Just as libraries do not endorse the viewpoints of those whose works are represented in their collections, libraries also do not endorse the beliefs or viewpoints of topics that may be the subject of library exhibits.

Exhibit areas often are made available for use by community groups. Libraries should formulate a written policy for the use of these exhibit areas to assure that space is provided on an equitable basis to all groups that request it.

Written policies for exhibit space use should be stated in inclusive rather than exclusive terms. For example, a policy that the library's exhibit space is open "to organizations engaged in educational, cultural, intellectual, or charitable activities" is an inclusive statement of the limited uses of the exhibit space. This defined limitation would permit religious groups to use the exhibit space because they engage in intellectual activities, but would exclude most commercial uses of the exhibit space.

A publicly supported library may limit use of its exhibit space to strictly "library-related" activities, provided that the limitation is clearly circumscribed and is viewpoint-neutral.

Libraries may include in this policy rules regarding the time, place, and manner of use of the exhibit space, so long as the rules are content-neutral and are applied in the same manner to all groups wishing to use the space. A library may wish to limit access to exhibit space to groups within the community served by the library. This practice is acceptable provided that the same rules and regulations apply to everyone, and that exclusion is not made on the basis of the doctrinal, religious, or political beliefs of the potential users.

The library should not censor or remove an exhibit because some members of the community may disagree with its content. Those who object to the content of any exhibit held at the library should be able to submit their complaint and/or their own exhibit proposal to be judged according to the policies established by the library.

Libraries may wish to post a permanent notice near the exhibit area stating that the library does not advocate or endorse the viewpoints of exhibits or exhibitors.

Libraries that make bulletin boards available to public groups for posting notices of public interest should develop criteria for the use of these spaces based on the same considerations as those outlined above. Libraries may wish to develop criteria regarding the size of material to be displayed, the length of time materials may remain on the bulletin board, the frequency with which material may be posted for the same group, and the geographic area from which notices will be accepted.

Adopted July 2, 1991, by the ALA Council.

ECONOMIC BARRIERS TO INFORMATION ACCESS: AN INTERPRETATION OF THE *LIBRARY BILL OF RIGHTS*

A democracy presupposes an informed citizenry. The First Amendment mandates the right of all persons to free expression, and the corollary right to receive the constitutionally protected expression of others. The publicly supported library provides free and equal access to information for all people of the community the library serves. While the roles, goals, and objectives of publicly supported libraries may differ, they share this common mission.

The library's essential mission must remain the first consideration for librarians and governing bodies faced with economic pressures and competition for funding. In support of this mission, the American Library Association has enumerated certain principles of library services in the *Library Bill of Rights*.

Principles Governing Fines, Fees, and User Charges

Article I of the *Library Bill of Rights* states: "Books and other library resources should be provided for the interest, information, and enlightenment of all people of the community the library serves.

Article V of the *Library Bill of Rights* states: "A person's right to use a library should not be denied or abridged because of origin, age, background, or views."

The American Library Association opposes the charging of user fees for the provision of information services that receive their major support from public funds. All information resources that are provided directly or indirectly by the library, regardless of technology, format, or methods of delivery, should be readily, equally, and equitably accessible to all library users.

Libraries that adhere to these principles systematically monitor their programs of service for potential barriers to access and strive to eliminate such barriers when they occur. All library policies and procedures, particularly those involving fines, fees, or other user charges, should be scrutinized for potential barriers to access. All services should be designed and implemented with care, so as not to infringe on or interfere with the provision or delivery of information and resources for all users. Services should be re-evaluated on a regular basis to ensure that the library's basic mission remains uncompromised.

Librarians and governing bodies should look for alternative models and methods of library administration that minimize distinctions among users based on their economic status or financial condition.

They should resist the temptation to impose user fees to alleviate financial pressures, at long term cost to institutional integrity and public confidence in libraries.

Library services that involve the provision of information, regardless of format, technology, or method of delivery, should be made available to all library users on an equal and equitable basis.

Charging fees for the use of library collections, services, programs, or facilities that were purchased with public funds raises barriers to access.

Such fees effectively abridge or deny access for some members of the community because they reinforce distinctions among users based on their ability and willingness to pay.

Principles Governing Conditions of Funding

Article II of the *Library Bill of Rights* states: "Materials should not be proscribed or removed because of partisan or doctrinal disapproval."

Article III of the *Library Bill of Rights* states: "Libraries should challenge censorship in the fulfillment of their responsibility to provide information and enlightenment."

Article IV of the *Library Bill of Rights* states: "Libraries should cooperate with all persons and groups concerned with resisting abridgments of free expression and free access to ideas."

The American Library Association opposes any legislative or regulatory attempt to impose content restrictions on library resources, or to limit user access to information, as a condition of funding for publicly supported libraries and information services.

The First Amendment guarantee of freedom of expression is violated when the right to receive that expression is subject to arbitrary restrictions based on content.

Librarians and governing bodies should examine carefully any terms or conditions attached to library funding and should oppose attempts to limit through such conditions full and equal access to information because of content. This principle applies equally to private gifts or bequests and to public funds. In particular, librarians and governing bodies have an obligation to reject such restrictions when the effect of the restriction is to limit equal and equitable access to information.

Librarians and governing bodies should cooperate with all efforts to create a community consensus that publicly supported libraries require funding unfettered by restrictions. Such a consensus supports the library mission to provide the free and unrestricted exchange of information and ideas necessary to a functioning democracy.

The Association's historic position in this regard is stated clearly in a number of Association policies: 50.4 Free Access to Information, 50.9 Financing of Libraries, 51.2 Equal Access to Library Service, 51.3 Intellectual Freedom, 53 Intellectual Freedom Policies, 59.1 Policy Objectives, and 60 Library Services for the Poor.

Adopted by the ALA Council, June 30, 1993.

EVALUATING LIBRARY COLLECTIONS: AN
INTERPRETATION OF THE *LIBRARY BILL OF RIGHTS*

The continuous review of library materials is necessary as a means of maintaining an active library collection of current interest to users. In the process, materials may be added, and physically deteriorated or obsolete materials may be replaced or removed in accordance with the collection maintenance policy of a given library and the needs of the community it serves. Continued evaluation is closely related to the goals and responsibilities of libraries and is a valuable tool of collection development. This procedure is not to be used as a convenient means to remove materials presumed to be controversial or disapproved of by segments of the community. Such abuse of the evaluation function violates the principles of intellectual freedom and is in opposition to the Preamble and Articles 1 and 2 of the *Library Bill of Rights*, which state:

The American Library Association affirms that all libraries are forums for information and ideas, and that the following basic policies should guide their services.

1. Books and other library resources should be provided for the interest, information, and enlightenment of all people of the community the library serves. Materials should not be excluded because of the origin, background, or views of those contributing to their creation.
2. Libraries should provide materials and information presenting all points of view on current and historical issues. Materials should not be proscribed or removed because of partisan or doctrinal disapproval.

The American Library Association opposes such "silent censorship" and strongly urges that libraries adopt guidelines setting forth the positive purposes and principles of evaluation of materials in library collections.

Adopted February 2, 1973; amended July 1, 1981, by the ALA Council.

ACCESS TO ELECTRONIC INFORMATION, SERVICES, AND NETWORKS: AN INTERPRETATION OF THE *LIBRARY BILL OF RIGHTS*

Introduction

The world is in the midst of an electronic communications revolution. Based on its constitutional, ethical, and historical heritage, American librarianship is uniquely positioned to address the broad range of information issues being raised in this revolution. In particular, librarians address intellectual freedom from a strong ethical base and an abiding commitment to the preservation of the individual's rights.

Freedom of expression is an inalienable human right and the foundation for self-government. Freedom of expression encompasses the freedom of speech and the corollary right to receive information. These rights extend to minors as well as adults. Libraries and librarians exist to facilitate the exercise of these rights by selecting, producing, providing access to, identifying, retrieving, organizing, providing instruction in the use of, and preserving recorded expression regardless of the format or technology.

The American Library Association expresses these basic principles of librarianship in its Code of Ethics and in the *Library Bill of Rights* and its Interpretations. These serve to guide librarians and library governing bodies in addressing issues of intellectual freedom that arise when the library provides access to electronic information, services, and networks.

Issues arising from the still-developing technology of computer-mediated information generation, distribution, and retrieval need to be approached and regularly reviewed from a context of constitutional principles and ALA policies so that fundamental and traditional tenets of librarianship are not swept away.

Electronic information flows across boundaries and barriers despite attempts by individuals, governments, and private entities to channel or control it. Even so, many people, for reasons of technology, infrastructure, or socioeconomic status do not have access to electronic information.

In making decisions about how to offer access to electronic information, each library should consider its mission, goals, objectives, cooperative agreements, and the needs of the entire community it serves.

The Rights of Users

All library system and network policies, procedures, or regulations relating to electronic resources and services should be scrutinized for potential violation of user rights.

User policies should be developed according to the policies and guidelines established by the American Library Association, including Guidelines for the Development and Implementation of Policies, Regulations and Procedures Affecting Access to Library Materials, Services, and Facilities.

Users should not be restricted or denied access for expressing or receiving constitutionally protected speech. Users' access should not be changed without due process, including, but not limited to, formal notice and a means of appeal.

Although electronic systems may include distinct property rights and security concerns, such elements may not be employed as a subterfuge to deny users' access to information. Users have the right to be free of unreasonable limitations or conditions set by libraries, librarians, system administrators, vendors, network service providers, or others. Contracts, agreements, and licenses entered into by libraries on behalf of their users should not violate this right. Users also have a right to information, training, and assistance necessary to operate the hardware and software provided by the library.

Users have both the right of confidentiality and the right of privacy. The library should uphold these rights by policy, procedure, and practice. Users should be advised, however, that because security is technically difficult to achieve, electronic transactions and files could become public.

The rights of users who are minors shall in no way be abridged. (See: Free Access to Libraries for Minors: An Interpretation of the *Library Bill of Rights*; Access to Resources and Services in the School Library Media Program; and Access for Children and Young People to Videotapes and Other Nonprint Formats.)

Equity Of Access

Electronic information, services, and networks provided directly or indirectly by the library should be equally, readily, and equitably accessible to all library users. American Library Association policies oppose the charging of user fees for the provision of information services by all libraries and information services that receive their major support from public funds (50.3; 53.1.14; 60.1; 61.1). It should be the goal of all libraries to develop policies concerning access to electronic resources in light of Economic Barriers to Information Access: An Interpretation of the *Library Bill of Rights* and Guidelines for the Development and Implementation of Policies, Regulations, and Procedures Affecting Access to Library Materials, Services, and Facilities.

Information Resources and Access

Providing connections to global information, services, and networks is not the same as selecting and purchasing material for a library collection. Determining the accuracy or authenticity of electronic information may present special problems. Some information accessed electronically may not meet a library's selection or collection development policy. It is, therefore, left to each user to determine what is appropriate. Parents and legal guardians who are concerned about their children's use of electronic resources should provide guidance to their own children.

Libraries and librarians should not deny or limit access to information available via electronic resources because of its allegedly controversial content or because of the librarian's personal beliefs or fear of confrontation.

Information retrieved or utilized electronically should be considered constitutionally protected unless determined otherwise by a court with appropriate jurisdiction.

Libraries, acting within their mission and objectives, must support access to information on all subjects that serve the needs or interests of each user, regardless of the user's age or the content of the material. Libraries have an obligation to provide access to government information available in electronic format. Libraries and librarians should not deny access to information solely on the grounds that it is perceived to lack value.

In order to prevent the loss of information, and to preserve the cultural record, libraries may need to expand their selection or collection development policies to ensure preservation, in appropriate formats, of information obtained electronically.

Electronic resources provide unprecedented opportunities to expand the scope of information available to users. Libraries and librarians should provide access to information presenting all points of view. The provision of access does not imply sponsorship or endorsement. These principles pertain to electronic resources no less than they do to the more traditional sources of information in libraries. (See: Diversity in Collection Development: An Interpretation of the *Library Bill of Rights*.)

Adopted by the ALA Council, January 24, 1996.

RESOLUTION ON THE USE OF FILTERING SOFTWARE IN LIBRARIES

WHEREAS, On June 26, 1997, the United States Supreme Court issued a sweeping re-affirmation of core First Amendment principles and held that communications over the Internet deserve the highest level of Constitutional protection; and

WHEREAS, The Court's most fundamental holding is that communications on the Internet deserve the same level of Constitutional protection as books, magazines, newspapers, and speakers on a street corner soapbox. The Court found that the Internet "constitutes a vast platform from which to address and hear from a world-wide audience of millions of readers, viewers, researchers, and buyers," and that "any person with a phone line can become a town crier with a voice that resonates farther than it could from any soapbox"; and

WHEREAS, For libraries, the most critical holding of the Supreme Court is that libraries that make content available on the Internet can continue to do so with the same Constitutional protections that apply to the books on libraries' shelves; and

WHEREAS, The Court's conclusion that "the vast democratic fora of the Internet" merit full constitutional protection will also serve to protect libraries that provide their patrons with access to the Internet; and

WHEREAS, The Court recognized the importance of enabling individuals to receive speech from the entire world and to speak to the entire world. Libraries provide those opportunities to many who would not otherwise have them; and

WHEREAS, The Supreme Court's decision will protect that access; and

WHEREAS, The use in libraries of software filters which block Constitutionally protected speech is inconsistent with the United States Constitution and federal law and may lead to legal exposure for the library and its governing authorities; now, therefore, be it

RESOLVED, That the American Library Association affirms that the use of filtering software by libraries to block access to constitutionally protected speech violates the Library Bill of Rights.

Adopted by the ALA Council, July 2, 1997.

Appendix D

Guidelines for the Development of Policies and Procedures Regarding User Behavior and Library Usage

INTRODUCTION

Libraries are faced with problems of user behavior that must be addressed to ensure the effective delivery of service and full access to facilities. Library governing bodies must approach the regulation of user behavior within the framework of the ALA Code of Professional Ethics, the *Library Bill of Rights* and the law, including local and state statutes, constitutional standards under the First and Fourteenth Amendments, due process, and equal treatment under the law.

Publicly supported library service is based upon the First Amendment right of free expression. Publicly supported libraries are recognized as limited public forums for access to information. At least one federal court of appeals has recognized a First Amendment right to receive information in a public library. Library policies and procedures that could impinge upon such rights are subject to a higher standard of review than may be required in the policies of other public services and facilities.

There is a significant government interest in maintaining a library environment that is conducive to all users' exercise of their constitutionally protected right to receive information. This significant interest authorizes publicly supported libraries to maintain a safe and healthy environment in which library users and staff can be free from harassment, intimidation, and threats to their safety and well-being. Libraries should provide appropriate safeguards against such behavior and enforce policies and procedures addressing that behavior when it occurs.

In order to protect all library users' right of access to library facilities, to ensure the safety of users and staff, and to protect library resources and facilities from damage, the library's governing authority may impose reasonable restrictions on the time, place, or manner of library access.

GUIDELINES

The American Library Association's Intellectual Freedom Committee recommends that publicly supported libraries use the following guidelines, based upon constitutional principles, to develop policies and procedures governing the use of library facilities:

1. Libraries are advised to rely upon existing legislation and law enforcement mechanisms as the primary means of controlling behavior that involves public safety, criminal behavior, or other issues covered by existing local, state, or federal statutes. In many instances, this legal framework may be sufficient to provide the library with the necessary tools to maintain order.
2. If the library's governing body chooses to write its own policies and procedures regarding user behavior or access to library facilities, services, and resources, the policies should cite statutes or ordinances upon which the authority to make those policies is based.
3. Library policies and procedures governing the use of library facilities should be examined carefully to insure that they are not in violation of the *Library Bill of Rights*.
4. Reasonable and narrowly drawn policies and procedures designed to prohibit interference with use of the facilities and services by others, or to prohibit activities inconsistent with achievement of substantial library objectives, are acceptable.
5. Such policies and the attendant implementing procedures

should be reviewed regularly by the library's legal counsel for compliance with federal and state constitutional requirements, federal and state civil rights legislation, all other applicable federal and state legislation, and applicable case law.

6. Every effort should be made to respond to potentially difficult circumstances of user behavior in a timely, direct, and open manner. Common sense, reason, and sensitivity should be used to resolve issues in a constructive and positive manner without escalation.

7. Libraries should develop an ongoing staff training program based upon their user behavior policy. This program should include training to develop empathy and understanding of the social and economic problems of some library users.

8. Policies and regulations that impose restrictions on library access:

   a. should apply only to those activities that materially interfere with the public's right of access to library facilities, the safety of users and staff, and the protection of library resources and facilities;

   b. should narrowly tailor prohibitions or restrictions so that they are not more restrictive than needed to serve their objectives;

   c. should attempt to balance competing interests and avoid favoring the majority at the expense of individual rights, or allowing individual users' rights to supersede those of the majority of library users;

   d. should be based upon actual behavior and not upon arbitrary distinctions between individuals or classes of individuals. Policies should not target specific users or groups of users based upon an assumption or expectation that such users might engage in behaviors that could disrupt library service;

   e. should not restrict access to the library by persons who merely inspire the anger or annoyance of others. Policies based upon appearance or behavior that is merely annoying or which merely generates negative subjective reactions from others, do not meet the necessary standard unless the behavior would interfere with access by an objectively reasonable person to library facilities and services. Such policies should employ a reasonable, objective standard based on the behavior itself;

f. must provide a clear description of the behavior that is prohibited so that a reasonably intelligent person will have fair warning and must be continuously and clearly communicated in an effective manner to all library users;

g. to the extent possible, should not leave those affected without adequate alternative means of access to information in the library;

h. must be enforced evenhandedly, and not in a manner intended to benefit or disfavor any person or group in an arbitrary or capricious manner.

The user behaviors addressed in these guidelines are the result of a wide variety of individual and societal conditions. Libraries should take advantage of the expertise of local social service agencies, advocacy groups, mental health professionals, law enforcement officials, and other community resources to develop community strategies for addressing the needs of a diverse population.

The American Library Association, January 24, 1993.

Appendix E

Policy on Confidentiality of Library Records

The Council of the American Library Association strongly recommends that the responsible officers of each library, cooperative system, and consortium in the United States:

1. Formally adopt a policy that specifically recognizes its circulation records and other records identifying the names of library users to be confidential in nature.*
2. Advise all librarians and library employees that such records shall not be made available to any agency of state, federal, or local government except pursuant to such process, order or subpoena as may be authorized under the authority of, and pursuant to, federal, state, or local law relating to civil, criminal, or administrative discovery procedures or legislative investigative power.

---

*Note: See also *ALA Policy Manual* 54.16, Code of Ethics, point 3, "Librarians must protect each user's right to privacy with respect to information sought or received, and materials consulted, borrowed, or acquired."

3. Resist the issuance of enforcement of any such process, order, or subpoena until such time as a proper showing of good cause has been made in a court of competent jurisdiction.**

Adopted January 20, 1971; revised July 4, 1975, July 2, 1986, by the ALA Council.

**Note: Point 3, above, means that upon receipt of such process, order, or subpoena, the library's officers will consult with their legal counsel to determine if such process, order, or subpoena is in proper form and if there is a showing of good cause of its issuance; if the process, order, or subpoena is not in proper form or if good cause has not been shown, they will insist that such defects be cured.

SUGGESTED PROCEDURES FOR IMPLEMENTING POLICY ON CONFIDENTIALITY OF LIBRARY RECORDS

When drafting local policies, libraries should consult with their legal counsel to insure these policies are based upon and consistent with applicable federal, state, and local law concerning the confidentiality of library records, the disclosure of public records, and the protection of individual privacy.

Suggested Procedures Include the Following:

1. The library staff member receiving the request to examine or obtain information relating to circulation or other records identifying the names of library users, will immediately refer the person making the request to the responsible officer of the institution, who shall explain the confidentiality policy.
2. The director, upon receipt of such process, order, or subpoena, shall consult with the appropriate legal officer assigned to the institution to determine if such process, order, or subpoena is in good form and if there is a showing of good cause for its issuance.
3. If the process, order, or subpoena is not in proper form or if good cause has not been shown, insistence shall be made that such defects be cured before any records are released. (The legal process requiring the production of circulation or other library records shall ordinarily be in the form of subpoena "duces tecum" [bring your records] requiring the responsible officer to attend court or the taking of his/her deposition and may require him/her to bring along certain designated circulation or other specified records.)
4. Any threats or unauthorized demands (i.e., those not supported by a process, order, or subpoena) concerning circulation and other records identifying the names of library users shall be reported to the appropriate legal officer of the institution.
5. Any problems relating to the privacy of circulation and other records identifying the names of library users which are not provided for above shall be referred to the responsible officer.

Adopted by the ALA Intellectual Freedom Committee, January 9, 1983; revised January 11, 1988.

POLICY CONCERNING CONFIDENTIALITY OF PERSONALLY IDENTIFIABLE INFORMATION ABOUT LIBRARY USERS: POLICY STATEMENT

The ethical responsibilities of librarians, as well as statutes in most states and the District of Columbia, protect the privacy of library users. Confidentiality extends to "information sought or received, and materials consulted, borrowed or acquired," and includes database search records, reference interviews, circulation records, interlibrary loan records, and all other personally identifiable uses of library materials, facilities, or services.

The First Amendment's guarantee of freedom of speech and of the press requires that the corresponding rights to hear what is spoken and read what is written be preserved, free from fear of government intrusion, intimidation, or reprisal. The American Library Association reaffirms its opposition to "any use of government prerogatives which lead to the intimidation of the individual or the citizenry from the exercise of free expression . . . [and] encourages resistance to such abuse of government power. . . . " (ALA Policy 53.4). In seeking access or in the pursuit of information, confidentiality is the primary means of providing the privacy that will free the individual from fear of intimidation or retaliation.

Libraries are one of the great bulwarks of democracy. They are the living embodiments of the First Amendment because their collections include voice of dissent as well as assent. Libraries are impartial resources providing information on all points of view, available to all persons regardless of age, race, religion, national origin, social or political views, economic status, or any other characteristic. The role of libraries as such resources must not be compromised by an erosion of the privacy rights of library patrons.

The American Library Association regularly receives reports of visits by agents of federal, state, and local law enforcement agencies to libraries, where it is alleged that they have asked for personally identifiable information about library users. These visits, whether under the rubric of simply informing libraries of agency concerns or for some other reason, reflect an insensitivity to legal and ethical bases for confidentiality, and the role it plays in the preservation of First Amendment rights, rights also extended to foreign nationals while in the United States. The government's interest in library use reflects a dangerous and fallacious equation of what a person reads with what that person believes or how that person is likely to behave. Such a presumption can and does threaten the freedom of access to information. It is also a threat to a crucial aspect of First Amendment rights: that freedom of speech and of the press include the freedom to hold, disseminate and receive unpopular, minority, "extreme" or even "dangerous" ideas.

The American Library Association recognizes that, under limited circumstances, access to certain information might be restricted due to a legitimate "national security" concern. However, there has been no showing of a plausible probability that national security will be compromised by any use made of *unclassified* information available in libraries. Thus, the right of access to this information by individuals, including foreign nationals, must be recognized as part of the librarians' legal and ethical responsibility to protect the confidentiality of the library user.

The American Library Association also recognizes that law enforcement agencies and officers may occasionally believe that library records contain information that would be helpful to the investigation of criminal activity. If there is a reasonable basis to believe such records are *necessary* to the progress of an investigation or prosecution, the American judicial system provides the mechanism for seeking release of such confidential records: the issuance of a court order, following a showing of *good cause* based on *specific facts*, by a court of competent jurisdiction.

Adopted July 2, 1991, by the American Library Association Council.

Appendix F

The Freedom to Read

The freedom to read is essential to our democracy. It is continuously under attack. Private groups and public authorities in various parts of the country are working to remove books from sale, to censor textbooks, to label "controversial" books, to distribute lists of "objectionable" books or authors, and to purge libraries. These actions apparently rise from a view that our national tradition of free expression is no longer valid; that censorship and suppression are needed to avoid the subversion of politics and the corruption of morals. We, as citizens devoted to the use of books and as librarians and publishers responsible for disseminating them, wish to assert the public interest in the preservation of the freedom to read.

We are deeply concerned about these attempts at suppression. Most such attempts rest on a denial of the fundamental premise of democracy: that the ordinary citizen, by exercising critical judgment, will accept the good and reject the bad. The censors, public and private, assume that they should determine what is good and what is bad for their fellow-citizens.

We trust Americans to recognize propaganda, and to reject it. We do not believe they need the help of censors to assist them in this task. We do not believe they are prepared to sacrifice their heritage of a free press in order to be "protected" against what others think may be bad for them. We believe they still favor free enterprise in ideas and expression.

We are aware, of course, that books are not alone in being subjected to efforts at suppression. We are aware that these efforts are related to a larger pattern of pressures being brought against education, the press, films, radio and television. The problem is not only one of actual censorship. The shadow of fear cast by these pressures leads, we suspect, to an even larger voluntary curtailment of expression by those who seek to avoid controversy.

Such pressure toward conformity is perhaps natural to a time of uneasy change and pervading fear. Especially when so many of our apprehensions are directed against an ideology, the expression of a dissident idea becomes a thing feared in itself and we tend to move against it as against a hostile deed, with suppression.

And yet, suppression is never more dangerous than in such a time of social tension. Freedom has given the United States the elasticity to endure strain. Freedom keeps open the path of novel and creative solutions, and enables change to come by choice. Every silencing of a heresy, every enforcement of an orthodoxy, diminishes the toughness and resilience of our society and leaves it the less able to deal with stress.

Now as always in our history, books are among our greatest instruments of freedom. They are almost the only means for making generally available ideas or manners of expression that can initially command only a small audience. They are the natural medium for the new idea and the untried voice from which come the original contributions to social growth. They are essential to the extended discussion which serious thought requires, and to the accumulation of knowledge and ideas into organized collections.

We believe that free communication is essential to the preservation of a free society and a creative culture. We believe that these pressures towards conformity present the danger of limiting the range and variety of inquiry and expression on which our democracy and our culture depend. We believe that every American community must jealously guard the freedom to publish and to circulate, in order to preserve its own freedom to read. We believe that publishers and librarians have a profound responsibility to give validity to that freedom to read by making it possible for the readers to choose freely from a variety of offerings.

The freedom to read is guaranteed by the Constitution. Those with faith in free people will stand firm on these constitutional guarantees of essential rights and will exercise the responsibilities that accompany these rights.

We therefore affirm these propositions:

1. It is in the public interest for publishers and librarians to make available the widest diversity of views and expressions, including those which are unorthodox or unpopular with the majority.

    Creative thought is by definition new, and what is new is different. The bearer of every new thought is a rebel until that idea is refined and treated. Totalitarian systems attempt to maintain themselves in power by the ruthless suppression of any concept which challenges the established orthodoxy. The power of a democratic system to adapt to change is vastly strengthened by the freedom of its citizens to choose widely from among conflicting opinions offered freely to them. To stifle every nonconformist idea at birth would mark the end of the democratic process. Furthermore, only through the constant activity of weighing and selecting can the democratic mind attain the strength demanded by times like these. We need to know not only what we believe but why we believe it.

2. Publishers, librarians, and booksellers do not need to endorse every idea or presentation contained in the books they make available. It would conflict with the public interest for them to establish their own political, moral, or aesthetic views as a standard for determining what books should be published or circulated.

    Publishers and librarians serve the educational process by helping to make available knowledge and ideas required for the growth of the mind and the increase of learning. They do not foster education by imposing as mentors the patterns of their own thought. The people should have the freedom to read and consider a broader range of ideas than those that may be held by any single librarian or publisher or government or church. It is wrong that what one can read should be confined to what another thinks proper.

3. It is contrary to the public interest for publishers or librar-

ians to determine the acceptability of a book on the basis of the personal history or political affiliations of the author.

A book should be judged as a book. No art or literature can flourish if it is to be measured by the political views or private lives of its creators. No society of free people can flourish which draws up lists of writers to whom it will not listen, whatever they may have to say.

4. There is no place in our society for efforts to coerce the taste of others, to confine adults to the reading matter deemed suitable for adolescents, or to inhibit the efforts of writers to achieve artistic expression.

   To some, much of modern literature is shocking. But is not much of life itself shocking? We cut off literature at the source if we prevent writers from dealing with the stuff of life. Parents and teachers have a responsibility to prepare the young to meet the diversity of experiences in life to which they will be exposed, as they have a responsibility to help them learn to think critically for themselves. These are affirmative responsibilities, not to be discharged simply by preventing them from reading works for which they are not yet prepared. In these matters taste differs, and taste cannot be legislated; nor can machinery be devised which will suit the demands of one group without limiting the freedom of others.

5. It is not in the public interest to force a reader to accept with any book the prejudgment of a label characterizing the book or author as subversive or dangerous.

   The ideal of labeling presupposes the existence of individuals or groups with wisdom to determine by authority what is good or bad for the citizen. It presupposes that individuals must be directed in making up their minds about the ideas they examine. But Americans do not need others to do their thinking for them.

6. It is the responsibility of publishers and librarians, as guardians of the people's freedom to read, to contest encroachments upon that freedom by individuals or groups seeking to impose their own standards or tastes upon the community at large.

It is inevitable in the give and take of the democratic process that the political, the moral, or the aesthetic concepts of an individual or group will occasionally collide with those of another individual or group. In a free society individuals are free to determine for themselves what they wish to read, and each group is free to determine what it will recommend to its freely associated members. But no group has the right to take the law into its own hands, and to impose its own concept of politics or morality upon other members of a democratic society. Freedom is no freedom if it is accorded only to the accepted and the inoffensive.

7. It is the responsibility of publishers and librarians to give full meaning to the freedom to read by providing books that enrich the quality and diversity of thought and expression. By the exercise of this affirmative responsibility, they can demonstrate that the answer to a bad book is a good one, the answer to a bad idea is a good one.

The freedom to read is of little consequence when expended on the trivial; it is frustrated when the reader cannot obtain matter fit for that reader's purpose. What is needed is not only the absence of restraint, but the positive provision of opportunity for the people to read the best that has been thought and said. Books are the major channel by which the intellectual inheritance is handed down, and the principal means of its testing and growth. The defense of their freedom and integrity, and the enlargement of their service to society, requires of all publishers and librarians the utmost of their faculties, and deserves of all citizens the fullest of their support.

We state these propositions neither lightly nor as easy generalizations. We here stake out a lofty claim for the value of books. We do so because we believe that they are good, possessed of enormous variety and usefulness, worthy of cherishing and keeping free. We realize that the application of these propositions may mean the dissemination of ideas and manners of expression that are repugnant to many persons. We do not state these propositions in the comfortable belief that what people read is unimportant. We believe rather that what people read is deeply important;

that ideas can be dangerous; but that the suppression of ideas is fatal to a democratic society. Freedom itself is a dangerous way of life, but it is ours.

This statement was originally issued in May of 1953 by the Westchester Conference of the American Library Association and the American Book Publishers Council, which in 1970 consolidated with the American Educational Publishers Institute to become the Association of American Publishers.

Adopted June 25, 1953; revised January 28, 1972, January 16, 1991, by the ALA Council and the AAP Freedom to Read Committee. A Joint Statement by: American Library Association and Association of American Publishers.

Subsequently endorsed by: American Booksellers Association, American Booksellers Foundation for Free Expression, American Civil Liberties Union, American Federation of Teachers AFL-CIO, Anti-Defamation League of B'nai B'rith, Association of American University Presses, Children's Book Council, Freedom to Read Foundation, International Reading Association, Thomas Jefferson Center for the Protection of Free Expression, National Association of College Stores, National Council of Teachers of English, P.E.N.-American Center, People for the American Way, Periodical and Book Association of America, Sex Information and Education Council of the U.S., Society of Professional Journalists, Women's National Book Association, and YWCA of the U.S.A.

Appendix G

Freedom to View

The following statement was adopted by the Intellectual Freedom Committee, American Library Association, June 1979:

The *Freedom to View*, along with the freedom to speak, to hear, and to read, is protected by the First Amendment of the Constitution of the United States. In a free society, there is no place for censorship of any medium of expression. Therefore, we affirm these principles:

1. It is in the public interest to provide the broadest possible access to films and other audiovisual materials because they have proven to be among the most effective means for the communication of ideas. Liberty of circulation is essential to ensure the constitutional guarantee of freedom of expression.
2. It is in the public interest to provide for our audiences films and other audiovisual materials which represent a diversity of views and expression. Selection of a work does not constitute or imply agreement with or approval of the content.
3. It is our professional responsibility to resist the constraint of labeling or pre-judging a film on the basis of the moral, religious, or political beliefs of the producer or filmmaker or on the basis of controversial content.
4. It is our professional responsibility to contest vigorously, by all lawful means, every encroachment upon the public's freedom to view.

This statement was originally drafted by the Educational Film Library Association's Freedom to View committee, and was adopted by the EFLA board of directors in February 1979.[1]

NOTE

1. *The Freedom to View* is not an American Library Association document, but it has been endorsed by ALA Council. The EFLA became the American Film and Video Association (AFVA).

Appendix H

Roles for Public Libraries

Introduction

The Public Library Association, as part of its Public Library Development Program, published *Planning & Role Setting for Public Libraries: A Manual of Options and Procedures* in 1987. The manual provides a planning process for public libraries to follow in defining the roles that the library will fulfill in providing service to the community. That manual also provides guidance for establishing goals and objectives for achieving excellent service and is essential reading for anyone planning to write or revise library policies. These roles were revised in April 1998 and are now called service responses. Regardless of the changes, these roles can help library policy makers define the primary functions the community expects their library to fulfill.

No library can meet all of the service needs that a community might desire. Limitations on budget, staff, and collection require that the library focus its resources on a manageable number of roles. "[C]hoices about service priorities not made deliberately are made by default."[1] The planning process described in *Planning and Role Setting for Public Libraries* guides staff and planners to direct "approximately 80% of the library's efforts . . . toward the primary and secondary roles."[2] "Roles not chosen for emphasis become maintenance roles. The remaining 20% of the library's effort supports these roles and other miscellaneous library activities."[3]

The Public Library Association, through the planning and role-setting process, identified eight general roles that encompass the contributions made by libraries to their communities. Other roles may be identified locally or the established roles may be modified to meet local needs. They are listed here as a starting point to aid policymakers in establishing policy. Bear in mind that there are no "better" roles and the roles are listed here in alphabetical order. The best roles are those that allow the library to provide the best service possible to meet the needs of the community it serves. It is strongly recommended that, as part of the overall planning process, policymakers will read the entire description of each role in the referenced manual and that the library's roles will be reviewed and revised on a regular basis.

PUBLIC LIBRARY ROLES[4]

Community Activities Center

The library is a central focus point for community activities, meetings, and services. The library provides both meeting room space and equipment for community- or library-sponsored programs. The facility is central to this role.

Community Information Center

The library is a clearinghouse for current information on community organizations, issues, and services. The library maintains a high profile as a source of information about community services. Users have a one-stop center to obtain current information about community organizations, issues, and services. The collection, including locally developed resources, and staff, skilled in reference and referral interviewing techniques, are central to this role.

Formal Education Support Center

The library assists students of all ages in meeting educational objectives established during their *formal* courses of study. The emphasis on registration for formal instruction distinguishes this role from the Independent Learning Center. Users find materials to supplement what is available in school or academic libraries (the library may decide to specify educational levels supported, i.e., elementary and secondary, but not postsecondary). The facility has space (study carrels) and equipment (typewriters, computers) to support students in completing school assignments.

Independent Learning Center

The library supports individuals of all ages pursuing a sustained program on learning independent of any educational provider. The staff help learners identify an appropriate learning path, determine needed resources, and obtain those resources from the library's collection or through interlibrary loan. Users can pursue self-determined and self-paced study on various subjects. The collection has a wide range of circulating subject materials, in a variety of formats, relevant to the interests of independent learners of all ages.

Popular Materials Library

The library features current, high-demand, high-interest materials in a variety of formats for persons of all ages. The library actively promotes and encourages the use of its collection. The collection includes current and popular materials in a variety of formats, with sufficient duplication to meet demand. A substantial percentage of the collection has been published within the past five years. The facility promotes browsing, has attractive display and good signage.

Preschoolers' Door to Learning

The library encourages young children to develop an interest in reading and learning through services for children, and for parents and children together. Services may include programs for infants, for parents and toddlers, and for parents. The library may provide outreach to daycare facilities. This role promotes lifelong use of the library and contributes to the library's image as an educational center for individuals of all ages. The staff are knowledgeable about early childhood development and children's literature.

Reference Library

The library actively provides timely, accurate, and useful information for community residents. The library promotes on-site and telephone reference/information services to aid users in locating needed information. Library users have convenient, timely access to information needed for daily living and decision making. The collection emphasizes information materials. The reference collection is extensive.

Research Center

The library assists scholars and researchers to conduct in-depth studies, investigate specific areas of knowledge, and create new knowledge. The library's collection, generally developed over a long period of time, is a source of exhaustive information in selected subject areas, which should be specified. The collection has a larger number of titles, extensive serials holdings, microform materials and equipment, a wide array of printed and electronic abstracting, indexing, and database services, and may include archival and manuscript materials.

NOTES

1. McClure, Charles R., et. al. *Planning & Role Setting for Public Libraries: A Manual of Options and Procedures.* Chicago, ALA, 1987, p. 28.
2. Ibid., p. 42.
3. Ibid., p. 42.
4. Ibid., pp. 28–39.

Bibliography

American Library Association. "Guidelines for the Development of Policies and Procedures Regarding User Behavior and Library Usage," January 24, 1993.

————. *Intellectual Freedom Manual*. 5th ed. Chicago: ALA, 1996.

————. "Policy on Confidentiality of Library Records." Adopted January 20, 1971; revised July 4, 1975, July 2, 1986, by the ALA Council.

————. "Suggested Procedures for Implementing Policy on Confidentiality of Library Records." Adopted by the ALA Intellectual Freedom Committee, January 9, 1983; revised January 11, 1988

Barlow, Richard. *Team Librarianship: The Advent of Public Library Team Structures*. London: Clive Bingley, 1989.

Baughman, James C. *Policy Making for Public Library Trustees*. Englewood, CO: Libraries Unlimited, 1993.

Bielefield, Arlene, and Lawrence Cheeseman. *Library Patrons and the Law*. New York: Neal-Schuman, 1995.

Boon, Belinda. *The CREW Method: Expanded Guidelines for Collection Evaluation and Weeding for Small and Medium-Sized Public Libraries*. Austin, TX: Texas State Library, 1995.

Bowen, Christopher. "Beyond Shhh! Developing the Discipline Policy of the Downers Grove Public Library." *Illinois Libraries* 70, no. 1 (January 1988): 25–32.

Cassell, Kay Ann, and Elizabeth Futas. *Developing Public Library*

Collections, Policies, and Procedures. New York: Neal-Schuman, 1991.

"Child Safety on the Information Highway." *http://www. missingkids. org/childsafety.html* (25 July 1997).

Crispen, Joanne L., ed. *The Americans with Disabilities Act: Its Impact on Libraries.* Chicago: American Library Association, 1993.

Curry, Betsy. *Georgia Public Library Trustees Handbook 1984.* Atlanta, GA: Georgia Library Trustees and Friends Association, 1984.

"Ethics Statement for Public Library Trustees." *Public Libraries* 24 (Winter 1995): 166.

Fidelman, Miles R. *All-Out Internet Access: The Cambridge Public Library Model.* Chicago: American Library Association, 1997.

Foos, Donald D., and Nancy C. Pack. *How Libraries Must Comply with the Americans with Disabilities Act (ADA).* Phoenix, AZ: Oryx, 1992.

"Four Tests for a Legally Enforceable Library Policy." *Library of Michigan Access.* 12 (September-October 1994): 9.

"Guidelines for Medical, Legal, and Business Responses at General Reference Desks." *RQ* 31, no. 4 (Summer 1992): 554–555.

"Guidelines for Multilingual Materials Collection and Development and Library Services." *RQ* 30, no. 2 (Winter 1990): 268–271.

Himmel, Ethel E. *Planning for Results: A Public Library Transformation Process.* Chicago: American Library Association, 1998.

Internet Librarianship. *http://www.rcls.org/libland/llinter.htm* (27 July 1997).

Intner, Sheila S. *Circulation Policy in Academic, Public, and School Libraries.* New York: Greenwood Press, 1987.

Karpisek, Marian. "Policy Writing." In *Policymaking for School Library Media Programs.* Chicago: American Library Association, 1989.

Kratz, Charles E., and Valerie Kratz. *The Personnel Manual: An Outline for Libraries.* Chicago: American Library Association, 1993.

"Latchkey Children" in the Public Library. Chicago: American Library Association, 1988.

Liddle, Carol. *Collection Development Plan for Janesville Public Library*. Janesville, WI: Janesville Public Library, 1994.

Loggins, Ann. *Library Policy Manuals: A Guide to Their Creation*. Ft. Worth, TX: North Texas Library System, 1989.

McClure, Charles R., et al. *Planning & Role Setting for Public Libraries*. Chicago: American Library Association, 1987.

Mayo, Kathleen, and Ruth O'Donnell, eds. *The ADA Library Kit: Sample ADA-Related Documents to Help You Implement the Law*. Chicago: American Library Association, 1994.

Million, Angela C., and Kim Fisher. "Library Records: A Review of Confidentiality Laws and Policies." *Journal of Academic Librarianship* 11, no. 6 (January 1986): 346–349.

Milo, Albert. "Ten Reasons Why We Buy Spanish Books." *Public Libraries* 5, no. 10 (November-December 1995): 340–341.

Molz, Kathleen Redmond. *Library Planning and Policy Making: The Legacy of the Public and Private Sectors*. Metuchen, NJ: Scarecrow Press, 1990.

Montgomery-Floyd Regional Library. *Internet Policy*. American Library Association, ala [Discussion List]. January 28, 1995.

Nichols, Margaret Irby. "The Reference Services Policy Manual." *Texas Library Journal* 63, no. 1 (Spring 1987): 30–32.

"One Lawyer's Opinion." *Texas Library Journal* 73, no. 2 (Summer 1997): 71.

PLA Handbook for Writers of Public Library Policies. Chicago: Public Library Association, 1993.

Policies & Procedures for the Public Library: A Sample Collection. Frankfort, KY: Kentucky Department for Library and Archives, 1985.

Policy Development Materials for Public Libraries. Hartford, CT: Connecticut State Library, 1995.

"Public Library Internet Access Policies." Lake Oswego (OR) Public Library. *http://www.ci.oswego.or.us/library/poli.htm* (25 May 1997).

Robbins, Jane. *Citizen Participation and Public Library Policy*. Metuchen, N.J.: Scarecrow Press, 1975.

Robbins, Jane Borsch. "Policy Formation in American Public Libraries: Effects of Citizen Participation." Ph.D. diss., University of Maryland, 1972 [c1973].

Rubin, Richard. "Ethical Issues in Library Personnel Management." *Journal of Library Administration* 14, no. 4 (September 1991): 1–16.

Sadowski, Michael J. "New St. Louis Policy Raises Questions of Parental Control." *School Library Journal* 40 (May 1994): 10.

Scholtz, James C. *Video Policies and Procedures for Libraries*. Santa Barbara, CA: ABC-CLIO, 1991.

Simon, Anne E., ed. *Kids Welcome Here! Writing Public Library Policies that Promote Use by Young People*. New York: New York Library Association, 1990.

Simpson, Carol Mann. *Copyright for School Libraries: A Practical Guide*. Worthington, OH: Linworth, 1994.

Sinclair, Dorothy. *Administration of the Small Public Library*. Chicago: American Library Association, 1979.

Smith, Mark. "Librarianship on the Bleeding Edge: Meeting the Pressure to Filter." *Texas Library Journal* 73, no. 2 (Summer 1997):74–77.

Stueart, Robert D., and Barbara B. Morgan. *Library Management*, 3rd ed. Englewood, CO: Libraries Unlimited, 1987.

————. *Library and Information Center Management*, 4th ed. Englewood, CO: Libraries Unlimited, 1993.

Stueart, Robert D., and Maureen Sullivan. *Performance Analysis and Appraisal*. New York: Neal-Schuman, 1991.

Symons, Ann. "Kids, Sex, and the Internet." *Texas Library Journal* 73, no. 2 (Summer 1997): 68–72.

Todaro, Julie B. *A Practical Guide for Personnel Management: The Essential Elements*, Austin, TX: Texas State Library, 1992.

Tryon, Jonathan S. *The Librarian's Legal Companion*. New York: G.K. Hall, 1994.

Turner, Anne M. *It Comes with the Territory: Handling Problem Situations in Libraries*. Jefferson, NC: McFarland, 1993.

Weingand, Darlene E. *Administration of the Small Public Library*. Chicago: American Library Association, 1992.

Weissman, Sara K. "Do You Dare?" *http://members.aol.com/saraweiss/access/index.html* (25 May 1997).

Williams, Lorraine M. *The Library Trustee and the Public Librarian: Partners in Service*. Metuchen, NJ: Scarecrow, 1993.

Index

A

Access to libraries, 153–156, 162–163
Advertisement of meetings held in the library, 127
ALA Intellectual Freedom Manual, 97
American Library Association, 6, 35–37, 68–70, 81, 119
  influence on policies, xv
Americans with Disabilities Act, xiii, 19, 49–51, 62
  self-evaluation plan, 50–51
  staff training, 50–51
Archival materials, 92–93
Art, donations of, 92
Association for Library Collections & Technical Services (ALCTS), 36

B

Behavior in the library, 183–186
Board of Trustees
  code of ethics, 36, 151
  meetings, 52

Bulletin boards, 132–134, 172–173

C

Challenged materials, 97, 161
Censorship
  relation to deselection of materials, 99
  trustees' role, 151
Certification of staff, 22–23
Children
  access to materials, 168–169
  access to services, 79, 108, 113, 121–122
  behavior, 139–142
  borrowers' cards, 70
  photocopies for, 112
Circulation
  records, 70
  statistics, 87
Code of ethics, 35–38, 69, 149–150
  trustees, 36, 151
Collecting fines and fees, 73–76
Collection development 85–88, 93
  diversity of materials, 166–167

plan, 86
Collection evaluation, 177
Communications Decency Act, 118–119
Community analysis, 93
Complaints about materials, 95–98, 99, 161
by non-residents, 97
Computer user agreements, 57
Confidentiality, 36, 66, 67–71, 75, 107
with regard to children's activities, 70
Constitution of the United States. 6, 161
Continuing education, 22–24
Copyright law, 79, 81–82, 110, 112
CREW Method: Expanded Guidelines for Collection Evaluation and Weed for Small and Medium-Sized Public Libraries, 99

D

Deselection of materials. *See* Weeding
Displays. *See* Exhibits and displays
Disposition of property, 100
Distribution of materials by staff, 43
Donations. *See* Gifts
Dress Code, 38–40

E

Electronic resources, 112–115, 178–181

Employees
benefits for, 27–29
hiring, 17–18
nepotism, 20–22
recruitment, 18–20
termination of employment, 32–34
Equal Employment Opportunity, 19
Equipment
donations of, 92
use by employees, 41
Exhibits and displays, 129–132, 172–173

F

Fair labor laws, 27, 31
Fees, 56, 65, 66, 72–76
for database searches, 114
for interlibrary loan, 79
for meeting room use, 127
for photocopies, 110, 112
non-residents, 66–67
relation to access to services, 72, 174–176
Freedom to read, 67, 193–198

G

Gifts, 88, 90–93
cost of donated materials, 90–91
of art, 92
of computer software, 56, 92
of equipment, 92
value of donated materials, 91

H

Homework assignments, 108–109

I

Intellectual freedom, 67, 95–98, 167, 193–198
Interlibrary loan. 77–80
Internet, 56, 57–61, 114
  filtering of, 119, 182
  training for patrons, 120–121
Internet access
  for patrons, 59, 116–117
  for staff, 57, 116

J

Job Accommodation Network, 19, 50

K

Kreimer, Richard, 137

L

Labeling
  of library materials, 159–160
Law enforcement agencies, 139, 184
Legal issues, xiii, xiv, 5–7, 69–71, 141, 146–147
  disposing of library property, 100
  related to library use, 66
Library Bill of Rights, 6, 97
Library hours, 53–55
Library programs, 61–63, 164–165

M

Materials
  labeling of, 159–160
  selection, 85–88
Meeting rooms, 42, 61–62, 125–129, 170–171

Microcomputers, 55–57
Morristown (NJ) Public Library, 137

N

National Center for Missing and Exploited Children, 122
Nationalities in the population, 93–95, 166–167
Nepotism, 20–22

O

Obscenity, 97
Office supplies
  patron use of, 144–145
Open meetings, 52
Overdue materials, 73–76

P

Patron complaints, 53
  about materials, 95–98
Patron registration, 65–67
Patron, participation in decision making, 51–53
Performance evaluation, 24–27
Photocopiers
  staff use, 41–42
Planning & Role Setting for Public Libraries, xviii, 49, 77, 87, 201–204
Policies
  and ALA, xv
  appealed policy, 4
  approval by governing authority, xvii, 13
  development of, xii, 4–5, 9–14
  externally imposed policy, 5, 6

implied policy, 5
length, xvi
local responsibility, xv, xvii
managerial policies, 1
operational policies, 2
originated policy, 4
validity test, 7
Policy manuals, 3, 14
Political activity. *See* Staff—
    Political Activity
Procedures, 2
Professional associations, 22,
    24
Public forum
    library as, 126, 132
    public meetings, 52
Public relations, 75

R

Reasonable accommodation,
    50
Reconsideration of materials,
    95–98
Reference services, 103–107,
    110
Religious holidays
    depicted in decorations,
        133–135
Resource sharing, 76–77, 87
Roles for Public Libraries. *See*
    Planning & Role Setting
    for Public Libraries
Rules of conduct, 137–139,
    183–186

S

Selection of materials
    clientele-oriented, 86

formats, 88, 92
Sexual harassment, xiii, 143
Sick leave, 29
Spanish language materials, 95
Special collections, 88, 93
Staff
    association, 44–45, 46
    book purchases, 44–45
    celebrations, 45–46
    development, 22–24
    political activity, 43–44
    sales in the library, 42–43
    use of library materials, 40–
        42
Staff training, 136–137
    regarding sexual harassment,
        143

T

Termination of Employment.
    See Employees-Termina-
    tion of Employment
Theft of materials, 146–147
Travel, 22–23
Trustees. *See* Board of Trustees

U

User fees, 174–175

V

Volunteers, 30–32, 53, 71, 91,
    105, 120–121

W

Weeding, 96, 99–101, 177

About the Authors

Jeanette Larson is the director of the Library Development Division at the Texas State Library and Archives Commission. In her previous position as manager of Continuing Education and Consulting Services for the Texas State Library, she presented or coordinated the presentation of more than 100 workshops each year for librarians, library staff, and library board members. She has worked in public libraries in Mesquite, Texas, and Anaheim, California. She received her M.S.L.S. from the University of Southern California. She is active in the American Library Association and in the Texas Library Association. In 1998, she was named Texas Library Association Librarian of the Year.

Herman L. Totten serves as associate dean and Regents Professor for the School of Library and Information Sciences at the University of North Texas in Denton, Texas. His previous positions include academic dean and librarian at Whiley College in Marshal, Texas; associate dean and associate professor at the University of Kentucky in Lexington, Kentucky; and dean and professor for the School of Librarianship at the University of Oregon in Eugene, Oregon. He has served as chair for the American Library Association's Committee on Accreditation, Minority Concerns Committee, Audiovisual Committee, and Information Science and Automation Division. He received the 1991 Association for Library and Information Science Education Award for Professional Contributions to Library and Information Science Education, and the 1992 American Library Association Black Caucus Award for Outstanding Contribution to the Field of Library and Information Science Education. He frequently presents workshops on library management and legal issues for the staff of small and medium-sized public libraries.